ACKNOWLEDGEMENT

I give honour to whom honour is due
Friend and Helper, Father/Daddy for His guidance and
wisdom whose love is un-conditional and everlasting.
It is because of His mercy that I was not consumed,
His compassion fails not and His grace is new every
day. Great is His faithfulness. Thank You Daddy for
Your ever present help in times of need and when I
am in trouble. I am glad God found me at the darkest
season of my life and turned that which the enemy of
my soul meant to cause me harm to beautify my life.
There were many things that could have stopped me
from writing this book but you were a step ahead of
them all. You go ahead of me and make every
crooked way straight. When I was weak and at the
verge of giving up, You stepped in for me and
shouldered me all the way. To the most amazing,
awesome, magnificent, incredible, dependable,
unwavering, uncommon, all knowing, all loving, all
perfect God, thank You!

I thank God for my children. It is not what I have done
for them that makes them a blessing to me but what
God has done in them and through them. It is an
honour and privilege to be chosen as a guardian
parent to them. I cherish them so much. To Ayomikun,
I am thankful for his encouraging words every step of
the way while writing this book, his constant reminder
that I can do all things through Christ who gives me
strength. Thank you for being there and being a good
listener during difficult times. I am thankful to Ayomide
for constantly checking on me throughout my
unending hours of writing and helping me with IT. His

confidence and a heart to do what he wants to do regardless of any obstacles have really stirred me to write this book. Am thankful to both for allowing me to be myself. I am not perfect and they accommodate my weaknesses. Thank you both for being part of my journey and allowing me to include you in this book. My prayer is that these precious boys of God will become men who will honour God. They will never forget what God has taught them, they will store His commands in their hearts and trust Him in good and bad times **(Psalms27:4-5).**

To my precious sister and friend Angela, I am thankful for the sleepless nights whilst proof reading this amazing book, for her sacrifices and time. Am grateful for her love and support throughout including the time I was recovering from sickness, was homeless and going through a divorce. I really appreciate our friendship and am grateful that she came alongside me in every project (elderly and connect group). Love her plenty. My gratitude to Eugene her husband and their two boys for including us into their family. I admire how Angela and Eugene have raised their children despite their busy life. I also admire their commitment and their wisdom around finance. I have really been blessed by the whole family and I am grateful to know them all **(Psalms133).**

To the man who taught me so much, my mentor, Mr Sunday Omotola Corker who I called brother Sunny. Thank you. I am grateful for all that you did and still doing for me. You are the man I will never forget. A man who believed in me when others did not. A man who clothed my nakedness when others exposed me.

A man who is only interested in one thing, to see me grow in the Lord and flourish in the spheres of my influence. Thank you for your caring heart. Through many years of separation and silence you are never forgotten. A man who is worth more than gold and silver. Your wife is blessed to have you as her husband and I pray that the God almighty that you serve will continue to grace you with more strength and wisdom in Yeshua's name; amen.

To my late father, John Olayinka Akintonde whose strength and weakness shaped me to be whom I am today. Though his life was cut short, his legacy lives on. I moaned about what he did not do for me when he was alive but writing this book has helped me see his positive side and to have an understanding of why he might have chosen his parenting style which I could not help but mentioned in the book.

Man

Ultimate journey of life

by Fehintola Akintonde

Printed in the United Kingdom

Unless otherwise indicates, Bible quotations are taken from The New International Version of the Bible

Other versions used are:
NASB,AMP,KJV,NKJV,MSG,AMPC,NLT,GNB

Twitter- @rest_wealth

Email – fehintolakitonde@gmail.com

To listen to the podcast covering some of the topics in this book, scan the code below using Spotify/anchor app.

Or use the link-
https://anchor.fm/s/1dbd1b14/podcast/rss

CONTENT

INTRODUCTION

The aim of this book is to challenge our young men to be fervent in their communication with God. I want them to understand who they are in Christ and flourish in all they do. Men are warriors and I believe it is important to direct that energy to something that will enhance their life. The book has two parts: what you need to know as a follower of Jesus Christ and how to use the knowledge in your everyday life. The book explains what prayer is and why it is essential. **Ephesians 6:12 says" For we wrestle not against flesh and blood, but against principalities, against powers, against the rulers of the darkness of this world, against spiritual wickedness in high places".** Many of us do not know how to pray or we pray based on our emotions or flesh **(James 4:3).** Many times what we want is not necessarily what we need. A 5 year old boy who asks his parent for a Ferrari is not being realistic and the closest he would get is a toy or souvenir Ferrari. So, in this book we learn about prayer and how to use it to get what we need.

The book also includes declarations/confessions to use to pray effectively. These will encourage, lift you up, give you hope and a future **(Revelation 12:11 "they overcame by the blood of the lamb and by the words of their testimony").** The power of life and death is in our tongue and we have the power to choose life. It is important that our words correspond with what we are praying for. We have to do our part and God will do His part. The words we say to ourselves matter and they will either build us up or pull us down. **"Truly I say to you, whoever says to this mountain, 'Be taken up and cast into the sea,' and does not doubt in his heart, but believes that what he says is going to happen, it will be granted him. Therefore I say to you, all things for which you pray and ask, believe that you have received them, and they will be granted you" (Mark 11:23-24NASB)**. The confessions are suitable for every season of life. They are personalised but they can also be used as cooperate prayers. The book also covers every stage of life. I want our young men to know that there is power when they pray and to be bold and confident when they approach God.

Prayer is not ancient, it is for all generations and the Lord hears every nation even though the way we pray may not be the same, the principle of prayer is still the same. My children say that I pray the African way which I do not dispute and I am grateful for the opportunity to have experienced a different culture which I can incorporate into my prayer. It is important to know we can bring anything to God no matter how small or big, silly or serious because He is interested in every detail of our lives. The book is a lifetime investment that will correct mistakes passed down from generations to generations. I recommend this book to young adults, men, parents, grandparents and all women who want to understand the men in their world. Sisters; the bible calls us helpers, so when you bless your brother or nephew with this book you are helping them.

If you desire to get married, this book will help you to gain more knowledge and understanding about who to marry, your role as a husband and a father God wants you to be. You can use the book as a study guide together with your fiancée, as believers sometimes do not know what to do with each other during courtship. Courtship time is not to be wasted on carnal things but to get to know each other. As much as it is exciting to talk about what you want to do together, how many children, how many cars or homes you want to have, it is also important to pray over your lives. I have heard ladies say; their fiancé does not like to pray together or everyone prays individually or there is no time to pray together. The greatest advice I can give you while courting is not to avoid praying together. The bible says where two people are gathered to pray, He is in the midst of them. You need God at the centre of your relationship. Pray together for the home you desire, the children God is bringing into your life and the kind of businesses, careers you both want to have. Pray and let God go ahead of you and make every crooked way straight. You need to make time for prayer at the beginning of your journey together. Find a comfortable time and your own way to pray. Remember this is about your relationship not about anyone else. As you begin this foundation with prayer, you will find out that it gets better and easier when you get married. Prayer will strengthen your marriage. You cannot pray too much or too little for your marriage. The earlier you start praying with your fiancée the earlier those burdens are being lifted and the Holy Spirit can reveal to both of you what areas of your life need urgent attention.

In my introduction, I referred to God as a Father, I understand this might be difficult for some readers because of their relationship with their earthly fathers. I do not mean to enhance your pain further but to help you deal with the issue and be free from that which wants to keep you bound for life. I pray that God will comfort you and heal your pain. Writing this book has helped me to reflect on my life, forgive and receive forgiveness from those I have hurt and those who have hurt me. The book has also helped me to reflect on my journey of faith, broaden my knowledge of God, renewed my approach towards life, inspired me and revived my prayer life. I have used the stories in the bible, my personal stories and friends/family's stories to express what I understand the Holy Spirit wanted me to share in this book. To be able to write this book, I have had to rely on the Holy Spirit to help me and I have seen His work in action every step of the way as new revelation kept coming each time I needed it. To God be the glory! Amen!

HOW TO USE THE BOOK

You can read the book as a study guide or on its own. Whichever way you chose to read the book, make sure you assimilate what each chapter is talking about and research further on anything that resonate with you or anything you do not understand. You can even journal about what you have learnt, changes you are going to make in your life, what you prayed for and how God answered the prayer. This is to remind you that God answers prayer next time you find yourself in similar/ tougher situations.

This book can be used as a self- assessment to improve your journey of faith. As I was writing it, I learnt quite a lot and gained insight in my areas of weakness. There are some chapters that I was not confident with but the Holy Spirit helped me. Every chapter has been influenced by the Holy Spirit which made it fun because if I had to write this with my knowledge it would not make sense. Each time I read the book, I learnt something new. So, as you read, pay attention to areas you struggle with and do not know anything about. Do your own studying; it will change your life.

There are some chapters that are longer than the other depending on what the Lord wants to convey to His people. If you ever feel stuck on a chapter and you do not feel like moving on to the next one, then stop and do more research of your own. Do not ignore this nudge! Talk to God about it and let Him show you what to do. For example, He might tell you to attend a course, volunteer in a specific area, study more, read books, listen to messages or go to bible school. This book can take you a month, a year or lifetime to read. As the bible is our manual for Godly principles, this book is there for us to understand some of those principles. The Holy Spirit is detailed and specific as I write each chapter. Read with an open mind and allow the Holy Spirit to help you understand the concepts.

Relax and enjoy the book.

WHAT IS PRAYER

Prayer is talking to God. Why do we talk to God? We talk to God because He created us in His image and He knows the answer to everything we need and want. He knew us from the beginning of creation and that is probably the reason He created all things before mankind. God placed man in a garden with all kinds of trees, to work and take care of it. Man could eat from any tree in the garden apart from the tree of the knowledge of good and evil. Mankind was given dominion to rule over everything that God created. God loves it when we talk to Him because He wants to relate with humanity. How do I know that? I have not seen God but I have seen how mankind relate with one another and enjoy each other's company and because we are created in God's likeness, I concluded He delights in our company, worship and praise. A perfect example I have is when my children were babies. As much as I loved my boys very much, their smile, cry, sleep and cuddles I loved it more when they could call me mum, ask me for something and we could have a conversation. No matter the situation surrounding a child at birth i.e. being pre-mature, disability; they are created in God's likeness. God loves us irrespective of how we came to the world, He sent Jesus to die for our sins, He is a faithful Father. Even though God knew us, before we were born, still He delights to hear our voices. **(Genesis 1; 1John 4; Ephesians2:19-22 MSG; Jeremiah 1:5).**

In 2020, there was a global pandemic (Covid19) which affected the way mankind related to each other. People had to maintain to 2 metres (3 steps) distance from each other. There was a lockdown where people could not go and visit their elderly parents and when they did, communication was through the window or in the driveway. If you happened to be admitted in the hospital, you were by yourself as relatives could not visit you. You were restricted as to where you could go and what you could do. You could not shake hands or hug your neighbours when you pass them in the corridor. You had to wear masks in order to communicate with friends and family when you were finally allowed to visit them. It was awkward and frustrating. Many found it difficult, suicide and mental health issues plummeted in our society. Lots of people died from the virus which brought pain and fear. And when the lock down was lifted, it felt weird at first because people did not know how to relate to one another. People were scared anxious as to what extent they could go to live their life again. Was Covid19 over or was it is still pre-eminent? The way we related as humans during the pandemic was compromised and it affected the way we functioned. When we refuse to talk to God, our relationship is compromised and we put ourselves at risk of walking outside His will. Humanity is created to have a relationship with the one who formed the earth and put everything in its right place.

If you do not know God or you have walked away from Him, there is no better time to reconnect back to God than now. He stands at the door of your heart today knocking, if you open the door He will come in regardless of what you have done and make things right with you **(Revlation3:20)**. The bible says "If my people, who are called by my name, will humble themselves and pray and seek my face and turn from their wicked ways, then I will hear from heaven, and I will forgive their sin and will heal their land" **(2Chronicles7:14)**. Say these words: Lord, I am sorry for my sin, I repent and I ask God to forgive me and come into my heart. Be my Lord and my Saviour. I have decided to follow You for the rest of my life in Jesus's name, Amen. Congratulations!!!!!!! If you made that commitment to follow Christ, I rejoice with you, in fact the host of Heaven rejoices with you **(Luke15:7)**. Heaven awaits you and your name has been written in the book of life. Welcome to the family of faith. Continue to get to know Him more!

Prayer is listening to God, it is a two way communication where we express ourselves to God in different ways and in return He responds to us. He wants to speak to us and He wants us to know about Him. It is important to listen and follow God's instructions when we pray. How do we do this? By reading the word of God and following the leading of the Holy Spirit. The bible says we pray and do not receive because our motives are wrong **(James4:3**) i.e. selfish desires (I want it and I want it for myself), manipulative prayer (If you don't do it for me I will die). **"Also, when you pray, do not be like the hypocrites; for they love to pray [publicly] standing in the synagogues and on the corners of the streets so that they may be seen by men. I assure you and most solemnly say to you, they [already] have their reward in full. But when you pray, go into your most private room, close the door and pray to your Father who is in secret, and your Father who sees [what is done] in secret will**

reward you (Matthew6:5-6). We do not pray only because we want something or when something is not going well in our life. Do not condition your prayer to only when you need it, you might be disappointed if your prayer is not answered. Maintain the relationship with your Father and you will be able to hear Him when He speaks to you.

Prayer is a personal way to communicate with our Father. The relationship God wants to have with us is inclusive not exclusive. The Lord wants us to be part of this relationship that is the reason He brought creatures to man, man offered his final verdict and so it was. **Now the Lord God had formed out of the ground all the wild animals and all the birds in the sky. He brought them to the man to see what he would name them and whatever the man called each living creature, that was its name. So the man gave names to all the livestock, the birds in the sky and all the wild animals (Genesis2:19-20).** You can talk to God about anything including secret things that no one knows or understand. He is the one that searches the heart and gives mankind the desires of their heart. You do not have to be perfect before Him, He knows about your imperfections and weaknesses **(Psalms103:14-16).** His ears are not too dull to hear you nor His arms too short that He cannot save you **(Isaiah59:1).** He is not like the world's network system or WI-FI that may fail us, He is always available to hear and answer our prayers. It is a direct line and you do not need a pastor/ priest to talk for you. We have an advocate, the Holy Spirit who supports our prayers and Jesus who intercedes for us before His Father. By talking to God and listening to

Him you will experience the relationship that God and Adam shared at the beginning of creation.

You can pray with other believers. Praying with other sisters and brothers in the body of Christ is our Heavenly Father's delight. I hear people say; why do I need to go to church if I can pray at home? There is power in co-operate prayer. Can you imagine what the Lord will do when His children get together to worship and exalt Him? The bible says where two or three people are gathered together in His name, He is in their midst and He will hear their prayers. **(Matthew 18:20}.** One of the greatest experiences of praying together was **"When the Day of Pentecost had fully come, they were all with one accord in one place. And suddenly there came a sound from heaven, as of a rushing mighty wind, and it filled the whole house where they were sitting. Then there appeared to them divided tongues, as of fire, and one sat upon each of them. And they were all filled with the Holy Spirit and began to speak with other tongues, as the Spirit gave them utterance"** **(Act2:1-4NKJV)**.

When someone asks you to pray for them, it is important to understand that it takes courage and boldness to share their vulnerability with you, so please respect and treat their information with confidentiality not gossip about it. Lots of people have missed their miracles because they refused to ask for prayer while some have kept their problems to themselves because of the way brothers and sisters in Christ have dealt with their story and information received in the past. Do not allow the ignorance of some people stop you from asking your fellow brothers and sisters to pray for you. We are not the same and our Father is still shaping all of us, so do not give up trusting people to pray for you if you have had bad experience with trust/confidentiality. Let the Lord lead you to people who will strength your faith and prayer.

How do we talk to God? Many people have talked about the time they have spent in praying for themselves or for others but I will say it is up to you how long you want to talk to God because He is your Father and He is interested in everything that concerns you. It is not how long you spend praying but how effective your prayer is. **"And when you pray, do not use meaningless repetition as the Gentiles do, for they think they will be heard because of their many words. So do not be like them [praying as they do]; for your Father knows what you need before you ask Him" (Matthew 6:7-8).** Live a lifestyle of prayer by praying in every season **(1 Thessalonians5:15-18).** When I started praying, I could only pray for 5 minutes and even with that I thought I had prayed for an hour. Then, gradually I began to tell my Father how much He meant to me and how I appreciate His presence in my life. I moved from only praying for myself to praying for my family, friends, colleagues, neighbours, employer, the government and nations. I have noticed that the more you spend time with your Father in prayer, the more inspiration He gives you and reveal to you things you do not know.

We can pray alone or with other believers, we can pray privately or as a cooperate body of Christ and we can pray quietly or aloud. However way we choose to pray, we need to bear in mind that our motive is what matters to God. We should pray with an honest heart, not to impress people or to show off how efficient we can pray. Pray in the spirit not in the flesh. There is no perfect way to pray to God, but there is only one way and that is through Jesus Christ **(John14:6).** When you pray you can close or open your eyes, whichever way you feel comfortable. I choose to close my eyes most of the time to avoid distraction but I have also opened my eyes when I am praying privately especially when my mind wonders off and needed to regain focus. Whichever way we pray, heaven will respond through provision, protection, guidance, wisdom, creativity, favour, opportunities, blessings, deliverance, revelation, health/wholeness, prosperity, abundance, revelation of the works of the enemy and give us insight into the heart of the father and more.

Above all pray in the Spirit on all occasions with all kinds of prayers and requests. With this in mind, be alert and always keep on praying for all the Lord's people. Pray also for me, that whenever I speak, words may be given me so that I will fearlessly make known the mystery of the gospel, for which I am an ambassador in chains. Pray that I may declare it fearlessly, as I should. (Ephesians6:18-20). The bible instructs us to pray in the spirit not in the flesh **(Romans8:1-32).** Praying in the flesh can be when we manipulate God in our prayers i.e. I will follow you for the rest of my life if you do that for me or when we ask Him to kill someone because we do not like them, we Want God to do things on our terms: you must do this for me by tomorrow. When the devil asked our Lord Jesus to fall down from the temple and God will send His angel to save Him, Jesus reminded the devil that he cannot tempt God **(Matthew4:5-7).** When we doubt God it displeases Him and He will not answer our prayer but if we believe, God is able to do what we are asking it will be done for us. Allow the Holy Spirit, which is the spirit of truth to guide you to pray. Rely on the Holy Spirit to pray for you and through you. When you pray in the spirit, miracles happen, signs and wonders follow our prayer and you will receive revelation of the word of God, dreams, visions and prophesy. When we pray in the spirit we are giving the Spirit permission to help us in the area of our weakness and the ability to express our words in prayer. The Spirit allows us to pray in unknown tongues(language) and the Father who knows all hearts knows what the Spirit is saying and will hear our prayer **(Romans 8:26-27)**

"But when the Helper (Comforter, Advocate, Intercessor—Counselor, Strengthener, Standby) comes, whom I will send to you from the Father, that is the Spirit of Truth who comes from the Father, He will testify and bear witness about Me .But you will testify also and be My witnesses, because you have been with Me from the beginning. (John 15:26-27AMP). The Spirit is what Jesus gave us when He went to His father. Jesus said the Holy Spirit would not come until He went back to the father, which means the Holy Spirit is as powerful as Jesus and the Father. They are called Trinity. God the Father, God the Son and God the Holy Spirit. The

Holy Spirit prays, intercedes for us, reveals the truth about the Father, testifies and bears witness about Jesus. The Holy Spirit will help, strengthen and counsel us. He is always on standby. You cannot get it wrong with the Holy Spirit. False prophets can tell you that "thou says the Lord" but it takes a discerning spirit to know the truth and that is why you need to be closer to the Holy Spirit so that you will not be deceived. **Matthew 7:15-19 says, "Beware of false prophets who come disguised as harmless sheep but are really vicious wolves. You can identify them by their fruit, that is, by the way they act. Can you pick grapes from thornbushes, or figs from thistles? A good tree produces good fruit, and a bad tree produces bad fruit. So every tree that does not produce good fruit is chopped down and thrown into the fire.**

Prayer is a spiritual experience. The flesh is always waging war with the spirit. You cannot have both, one wins and one is defeated. When we pray in the Spirit, we invite the Holy Spirit to take control and do what we cannot do. The Holy Spirit will take you to territories where your enemies are afraid of you. The demon begged Jesus to send them to the herd of pigs **(Matthew8:31).** The Holy Spirit will guide, refresh you and make things happen for you. He will give you boldness you do not think you have, help you to step out of your comfort zone and make decisions that are beyond your wildest dream. The Holy Spirit will go ahead of you and make every crooked way straight and reveal hidden things about the Father and show you things to come. To close a business deal or go into a business partnership you will need the Holy

Spirit to help you so that you do not lose money, sleep, or assets. I always pray that Yahweh will give me the eyes of the sprit to see what Yahweh sees, to love what He loves and hate what He hates. The Spirit of the Sovereign Lord is available to everyone who receives Jesus as their Lord and saviour. Prayer is the key to unlock doors of miracles, favours and opportunities. Pray without ceasing. Pray in every season. Pray until you see the manifestation in your life

PRAYER AND CONFESSION

My Heavenly Father, I am grateful that I can talk to You and express my concerns to You in prayer. Help me to pray with humbleness of heart not pride or arrogance.

I thank Yahweh that I can come to Him at anytime and anywhere. I do not need someone to speak to my father on my behalf.

May my life reflect Jesus - the way, the truth and life. **(John 14)**

Father, remove anything that does not resemble Your image or likeness in my life. Any habit, attitude, behaviour that does not speak of You, take it away Lord. Jesus is the real vine, and His Father is the gardener. He breaks off every branch in me that does not bear fruit, and He prunes every branch that does bear fruit in me ,so that it will be clean and bear more fruit **(John15:1-2).**

Father, You are the best teacher, teach me how to pray. May I pray according to Your will, not my will and be led by the Spirit

When I ask, I will receive, when I seek God, I will find him and when I knock, the door will be opened for me **(Matthew7:7)**

I receive the hunger to pray at all times and in every season.

I will come boldly to obtain favour from Your presence. I will enter Your gates with thanksgiving, Your court with praise and I will say this is the day the Lord has made and I will rejoice in it.

I love to pray for others and I will not forsake the gathering of believers that call upon the name of Jesus **(Hebrews10:25)**

I will allow the Holy Spirit to direct my words in prayer so that my motives and attitudes are right and acceptable to God.

I understand that there is power of life and death in my mouth but I choose to speak life to every raging storm in my life.

Help me Holy Spirit to create time to talk to God, listen to Him, meditate on His word and apply the word of God in prayer.

Jesus was never tired of prayer. I will not be tired of prayer.

I receive the anointing to proclaim good news, bind up the broken hearted, free those in captive, release from prison those bound, comfort those who mourn, give beauty instead of ashes, joy for mourning and praise instead of the spirit of despair **(Isaiah61:1-3).**

I will always acknowledge my Heavenly Father and not lean on my own understanding but reverence and declare that You are the Lord of my Life **(Proverbs3:5-6).**

JESUS OUR GREATEST EXAMPLE OF PRAYER: TAUGHT PRAYER

Jesus is our great example when it comes to prayer. He was seen praying privately and with people. He demonstrated His intimacy with His father. As Jesus was praying in a certain place, one of His disciples asked Him to teach them how to pray **(Luke11:1).** I find this as a foundation to prayer so if you are struggling to pray or you do not know what to say when praying, start with the Lord's Prayer -

"Our Father in heaven, hallowed be Your name. Your kingdom come, Your will be done on earth as it is in heaven. Give us this day our daily bread. And forgive us our debts, as we forgive our debtors. And do not lead us into temptation, but deliver us from the evil. For Yours is the kingdom and the power and the glory forever. Amen."(Matthew 6:7-13 NKJV)

Let us look at the Lord's Prayer:

"Our Father in Heaven"

In this scripture, we see that Jesus started His prayer by acknowledging His father. In the world that will live in, where there are so many gods, you need to differentiate who you are praying to. God said He will not share His glory with any one **(Isaiah 42:8).** Jesus made praying to His Father personal, He was not talking to God as a stranger but as His Father. I do understand that for some of us, our relationship with our earthly fathers might not be great but we have a

Father who is greater than our earthly father. You cannot approach the heavenly Father the way you approach your earthly father especially if you did/do not have a personal relationship with him.

I have known the Lord for a while but I did not have this relationship with Him until I was in my late 30's. I was having a conversation with my connect group leader about my relationship with God and why I was struggling to relate to the Father the way I should. She asked me about my relationship with my earthly father and she said it might be that I am relating to my Father based on the fathers I have seen or known. At first it did hurt because I have known the Lord for a while but I went home and began to articulate the way I relate with God. My earthly father (late) was an absent father, broke his promises many times and if we were left in the room by ourselves we would have nothing to say to each other. I realised that I have based my relationship with God on how my earthly dad was with me. This realisation changed my perspective of who my Heavenly Father is and He became my Father not just some guy in Heaven but the one who loves me the way I am. Your father might be perfect or he might be like mine but I want you to know that your Heavenly Father will never leave or forsake you, He is with you yesterday, today and will be with you tomorrow. As a father has compassion on his children so the Lord has compassion on those who fear Him. As high as the heavens are above the earth so great is His love for those who fear Him **(Psalms103:11-13).**Embrace the Father's love today and let it transform you into the image He created you to be. Your Father who is in Heaven will do for you what your earthly father cannot do for you. **Romans 8:29-30 says: Those whom God had already chosen he also set apart to become like his Son, so that the Son would be the eldest brother in a large family. And so those whom God set apart, he called; and those he called, he put right with himself, and he shared his glory with them (GNB).** He is the only one who will not disappoint or judge you.**Ephesians1: 4-7 says: Even before the world was made, God had already chosen us to be his through our union with Christ, so that we would be holy and without fault before him. Because of his love God had already decided that through Jesus Christ he would make us his sons and daughters — this was his pleasure and purpose. Let us praise God for his glorious grace, for the free gift he gave us in his dear Son! For by the blood of Christ we are set free, that is, our sins are forgiven. How great is the grace of God (GNB).**

"Hallowed be your name"

It is good to worship God who makes all things beautiful. **Bless the Lord oh my soul and all that is within me bless the holy name. Bless the Lord oh my soul and forget not all his benefit (Psalms103:1-2).** This is the best time to express how much you love Him and what He means to you. Sing to Him love songs because He inhabits the praises of His people **(Psalms22:3 KJV).** Tell Him how much you appreciate His presence, His love and His working power in your life. Thank God for His presence that is full of joy, peace, healing and pleasurable ever more **(Psalms16:11).** I remember years ago when I got a sister's name wrong (I am human after all don't blame me) she was upset and I had to apologise for days before she could forgive me, she even referred to it from time to time in our conversations. The Father loves us regardless of our failings and His son's death wiped away our sins while we were yet sinners **(Romans5:8-10).** So, therefore praise the name of Jesus that brought you freedom, liberty, redemption and salvation for without Him it is impossible to please God. Thank His name that showed us the way, the truth, the life and the assurance that when we call on the name He will hear us. Let the smelling aroma from praising His name make it impossible for Heaven to ignore you. Praise His holy name.

"Your kingdom come, Your will be done on earth as it is in Heaven."

God's Kingdom is His presence and it is important to invite Him into our life to take control and be the centre of our life. Invite His presence to come and give us guidance, direction, wisdom and insight into the circumstances surrounding our life. For He said in **Revelation3:20** that He stands at the door and knock and if anyone hears His voice and open the door, He will come into their life. When we open our mouth to pray, we want our words to bring His kingdom on earth, we speak words that bring life and hope to humanity. His kingdom is about love and our Love for Him must be to love what He loves and care about what He cares about. Our prayer should reflect who He is and His kingdom by creating time to spend with the Father as Jesus constantly did. When Jesus was about to be crucified, He knelt down and prayed; **"Father, if thou be willing, remove this cup from me: nevertheless not my will, but thine, be done" (Luke22:42, Matthew26:39).** When we pray, it is important to allow Him to do what we cannot do with our power and surrender our will, thoughts, body, soul and spirit to Him. Come to His presence with Heaven in mind and be prepared to receive an answer to your prayers. A boy who goes to the exam room with nothing to write will not do well. Do not go to God with demands; allow His will to be done in your life.

"Give us this day our daily bread."

It is God's promise to supply all our needs according to His riches in glory. He is our shepherd and we will lack nothing **(Psalms23:1).** He provided everything that mankind needed before creating mankind because He knows what we need and He will not withhold any good thing from those who walk uprightly with Him. **(Psalms84:11).** We know and believe that when we ask it will be given to us, even though our Heavenly Father knows all things and can do all things." **For everyone who asks receives; he who seeks finds; the one who seeks finds and to the one who knocks, the door will be opened" (Matthew7:8).** Do not limit what God can do for you, your family and friends. There is nothing too small or too big that our Father cannot do for His children, so do not be afraid to ask for anything. Notice Jesus only asked for our daily bread, this is so that we can be content and grateful for what He has done and what He will do each day.

The bible says we should not worry about what we will eat, drink or wear, for our heavenly Father will provide: **"Therefore I tell you, do not worry about your life, what you will eat or drink; or about your body, what you will wear. Is not life more than food, and the body more than clothes? Look at the birds of the air; they do not sow or reap or store away in barns, and yet your heavenly Father feeds them. Are you not much more valuable than they? Can any one of you by worrying add a single hour to your life? "And why do you worry about clothes? See how the flowers of the field grow. They do not labor or spin. Yet I tell you that not even Solomon in all his splendour was dressed like one of these. If that is how God clothes the grass of the field, which is here today and tomorrow is thrown into the fire, will he not much more clothe you—you of little faith? So do not worry, saying, 'What shall we eat?' or 'What shall we drink?' or 'What shall we wear?' For the pagans run after all these things, and your heavenly Father knows that you need them. But seek first his kingdom and his righteousness, and all these things will be given to you as well. Therefore do not worry about tomorrow, for tomorrow will worry about itself. Each day has enough trouble of its own (Matthew6:25-34).**

"And forgive us our debts, as we forgive our debtors."

We are human and the Lord knows we will get things wrong, He is not expecting perfect beings, He is interested in our obedience and trust in Him. **"The Lord is compassionate and gracious; slow to anger and abounding in love. He will not always accuse, nor will he harbour his anger forever. He does not treat us as our sins deserve or repay us according to our iniquities" (Psalms103:8-10).** Whilst Jesus was dying on the cross, He prayed for the people who betrayed and denied Him. He told His Father to forgive them for they didn't know what they were doing. If the Lord could do that how much more should we forgive those who hurt us? I learnt a few years ago that If I can offend people and I want them to forgive me, I must also be prepared to forgive those who offend me. This realisation changed my concept of forgiveness. When we ask God to forgive us, we are not only asking for things we have done wrong but things we have also not done wrong in our sight, for God is the only one who judges what is right and wrong. The Lord wants you to confess your sins to Him and He will forgive you. The enemy wants to hold your sins against you in order to accuse you every time you approach God's presence. Confess the sins you have committed knowingly and unknowingly, the sins in your consciousness and sub-consciousness, sins you have committed in your actions, thoughts, mind, attitude and habits you have picked up that do not honour and glorify God. David said 'search me oh Lord and know my heart' **(Psalms139),** ask the Lord to search your heart and reveal to you what needs to change.

"And do not lead us into temptation, but deliver us from the evil."

Temptation is a desire to do something wrong and unwise. As believers, we have the Holy Spirit inside us to convict us if we are doing something wrong or going the wrong direction. For example, I have been told by the Holy Spirit in the past to do something as simple as picking up my litter when I dropped it on the floor. As much as I did not want to do it and my attitude did suck, I obeyed the Spirit of God and now I have become a good citizen in my community to the glory of God. When the Holy Spirit corrects us, it is for our benefit depending on what He is doing in the season of our life. Temptation is not a sin, it is what we do about it that matters and that is the reason we need to pray that God should lead us not into temptation, for the heart of humanity is desperately wicked **(Jeremiah17:9-10)** and we need to constantly renew our mind and abstain from evil.

Therefore, I urge you, brothers and sisters, in view of God's mercy, to offer your bodies as a living sacrifice, holy and pleasing to God this is your true and proper worship. Do not conform to the pattern of this world, but be transformed by the renewing of your mind. Then you will be able to test and approve what God's will is, his good, pleasing and perfect will (Romans 12:1-2). A father who chooses to beat his son everyday might think he is doing the boy a favour so that as he grows up, his behaviour will change but we have seen that this is not necessarily true. For some it makes them hate their father, run away from home, rebellious, resentful and bitter. The Lord is the only one who can lead us not into temptation and deliver us from evil and as a parent himself He knows the right ways to handle stiff necked people **(Act7:51).**

"For Yours is the kingdom and the power and glory forever."

Yours is the kingdom: Anyone who acknowledges God through His son Jesus is guaranteed this kingdom **(Ephesians1; 2; 3).** The kingdom of Heaven is not when we get there, we can experience His kingdom while on earth. Do not postpone your joy till when you get to Heaven but enjoy His kingdom, glory and power on earth.

Yours is the power: All power and glory belong to God. He has the power and authority to heal, deliver and set us free and He has given that power to those who call upon His name **(Luke4:18, Isaiah61:1).** He has also given us power and authority to tread on serpents and scorpion and over all the power of the enemy and nothing shall hurt us **(Luke 10:19).** Only our Father can give power that will add no sorrow. Saul in his quest for power ended up disobeying God and the glory of the Lord departed from him **(1Samuel13-15).**

Yours is the glory forever: Glory is used to describe the manifestation of God's presence, His greatness and who He is **(Exodus24:9-11).** In God's marvellous glory and excellence, He gave us all we need and called us to Himself **(2Peter1:3).** His glory is for Him alone and He will not share it with anyone

(Isaiah42:8). When His glory descends on His people there are blessings and miracles. His glory rules over His people and no one can withstand Him or stand against Him **(2 Chronicles20:6).** He is the God without comparison. The glory of God cannot be ignored for it is seen by all men. The children of Israel were afraid to approach Moses when he came down from Mount Sinai after meeting with God **(Exodus 19&34:29-35).** Sin cannot withstand the glory of God. We give glory to the one who is able to do more than we ask or think by His mighty power at work in us **(Ephesians3:20)** These three things are what believers enjoy when they acknowledge God as our Lord and Saviour. May His kingdom, His Power and His Glory rest upon us forever and ever. Amen

"Amen"

I see amen as a full stop to a sentence. In other words, there is nothing to add or take away from it. When I say amen at the end of my prayers, I am declaring that what I have asked will be a reality in my life. When we say amen at the end of our prayers, we acknowledge that it is done even though we have not seen it yet. This is faith in action and the bible says if we have faith as small as a mustard seed, what we ask will be done for us. On the cross, Jesus said it is finished, in other words He had completed His work on earth and humanity just needs to receive it. Amen is receiving the promises God promised through His son. If I asked you whether you want £1000 and you do not say yes or stretch your hands forward to receive the money or give me a facial gesture, I will assume you do not want the money. I see amen as a stamp/ signature that endorses something; a final say. So when you pray or when someone prays for you it is important to say amen.

JESUS'S DEMONSTRATION OF PRAYERS

Jesus prayed in the garden of Gethsemane: **Matthew 26:36-46**

Jesus prayed alone: **Mark 1:35-46, Luke 9:18, Luke 22:39-41**

Jesus prayed in public**: John 11:41-42**

Jesus prayed when His soul was troubled: John **12:27-30**

Jesus prayed before meals: **Matthew 26:26, Mark8:6, Luke 24:30**

Jesus prayed before/after healing**: Mark 7:34-35; Luke5:16**

Jesus prayed to do His Father's Will: **Matthew26:36-44**

Jesus taught the importance of prayer**: Matthew 21:22;5:44; 6:5**

Prayer at His Baptism: **Luke3:21-22**

Jesus prayed before heading out: **Mark1:35-36**

Jesus prayed all night before choosing his disciples**: Luke6:12-13**

Jesus prayed while speaking to Jewish leaders: **Matthew11:25-26**

Jesus gave thanks to the father: **John6:11, Matthew15:36**

Jesus prayed for himself, disciples and all believers: **John17:1-26**

Jesus prayed for the sick:**Luke7:1-10; 8:26-39, Mark5:1-20;2:1-12**

Jesus prayed for the children: **Matthew19:13**

Jesus prayed on the cross: **Luke23:34; Matthew27:46,**

As Jesus was preparing for His death, He prayed to the Father to protect the believers and those that will be saved when He goes back to the Father**: "Keep them safe", "protect them" "and let none of them be lost except the one bound to be lost", "Keep them safe from the evil one", "Dedicate them to Yourself by means the truth of Your word", "I dedicated Myself to You, in order that they too may be truly dedicated to You", "I pray they that they may all be one", "Father! May they be in Us, just as You are in me and I am in You", "May they be one, so that the world will believe You sent Me", "I in them and You in Me, so that they may be completely one, in order that the world may know You sent Me and that You love them as You love Me", "Father! You have given them to Me, and I want them to be with Me where I am, so that they may see My glory, the glory You gave Me" John17 NIV**

PRAYER AND CONFESSION

I thank Jesus for teaching me how to pray, You did not just leave me to figure it out by myself. You know I might struggle in this area and You made provision for it. Even though You are God yourself, You never ceased to acknowledge and reverence Your Father.

Jesus is my greatest example of prayer, may I follow in His footsteps and live a lifestyle of prayer, I will pray at all times and in every season and I will express my love, worship, gratitude, praise, communion to God

Forgive my sins and those who have in their heart to harm me. Let me forgive those who have offended me as I know I have offended others too and may the people I have offended find it in their heart to forgive me. Lead me not into temptation but deliver me from the evil one

Jesus the light of the world, shine Your light on my path **(John1)**

I ask that You will renew my emptiness and turn my shame into dancing.

Every time Jesus prayed signs and wonders followed. Father, let signs and wonders follow my prayers **(John2)**

Jesus our salvation, always loving people and saves those the Father gives to Him, I pray for salvation of my friends, family, neighbour, colleague, employer, employee and above all those who despise me without a cause **(John3).**

Jesus the living water, quenches my thirst O Lord! (**John4**)

Jesus the deliverer, deliver me from prolonged sickness, that has lingered for so long, situations that have paralyzed and crippled me physically, emotionally and spiritually (**John5**)

Jesus the Bread of life, Breathe life to every dead situation in my life (**John6**)

Jesus, give me wisdom and discernment to do the right thing. I receive knowledge, understanding, discretion and intellect that amazes my enemy, friends and even myself. I will thirst and hunger for Your word and the word I speak will align with Heaven (**John7**)

Jesus my defence, be my defence when I am accused wrongly and rebuke the devil's schemes. As the accuser of the brethren (satan) goes about looking for those he will devour, I will not be subjected to his devices. The Lord will fight my battle and I will be still. Jesus intercedes for me and silence the plans of the enemy (**John8**)

Jesus prayed for the sick and they received their healing. I receive the boldness to pray for healing. (**John9**)

Help me to hear and recognise when You speak to me. The voice of the strangers, I will not follow and I will not seek man made power and any power that elevates itself above/against the most high God. I will serve no foreign god or any other treasures. The Lord's will is my heart desire and His spirit is my pleasure (**John10**)

Jesus was always moved with compassion to pray for people. I will always be moved by compassion to pray for the poor and under privileged. I will emphasise when others are going through a tough time and intercede for them in prayer.

Jesus the resurrection, resurrect every dead dream and ambition. Cause me to laugh again. (**John11**).

Jesus the anointed one, fill me with the fragrance of Your presence that attracts people to know You I receive boldness to operate in the anointing God placed on my life and I will not doubt. May Your anointing renew, refresh, and restore me (**John12**)

As You wash the feet of Your disciples, wash & cleanse me from all unrighteousness and create a clean heart in me (**John13**)

TYPES OF PRAYER

There are different ways we can express ourselves in prayer. There is no methodology for this, pray as the Holy Spirit leads you. Here is some guidance;

PRAYER OF BLESSINGS OVER OUR LIFE: This prayer is to receive and affirm the blessings God has promised those who believe in Christ the son of God and acknowledge what He has done for us even before we ask Him. The blessing of God that has been established in Heaven is waiting for earth (You and I) to claim it. God is not thinking about what to do when we place our requests before Him, He already knows the answer. The bible says while we were yet sinners Christ died for us **(Romans5:8).** He does not change His mind like human beings; He is the same yesterday, today and forever more. God's blessings are not a result of what you have done but what He did for you. There are some blessings you do not deserve that He made available to you. Every blessing is unique and God deserves to be praised for it. We sing "Abraham's blessings are mine" because God blessed Abraham and was accredited to him **(James2:23)**. Receive every blessing that heaven is pouring upon the face of the earth today. **Bless the Lord o my soul and all that is within me bless his holy name, Bless the Lord o my soul and forget not all his benefit. Who forgives all my iniquities, heal my diseases, redeem my life from destruction, crown me with lovingkindness and tender mercies, satisfy my mouth with good things**

and renew my youth like the eagle(Psalms 103:1-5).

PRAYER OF THANKSGIVING: O give thank onto the Lord for He is good and His mercy endure for ever. Thank God with all your heart. Do not give a partial sacrifice of thanksgiving that is not accepted like Cain **(Genesis4:5).** A grateful heart opens doors for more blessings. Give thanks to God in every season and in all circumstances. Appreciate what the Father has done, what He is doing and what He will do for you. Thank Him for the things you have prayed for and you have not seen come to pass. Thank Him until you receive your breakthrough. Do not let your thanksgiving be known only when God has done something for you. Human nature is always to receive but we forget to give thanks to the one who gives the blessings. It is easy to promise heaven and earth when you are believing God for something but we tend to forget our promises when the breakthrough comes. Do not forget or ignore your vow to God but give Him what is due to Him. **Give and it shall be given to you, good measure pressed down, shaking together and running over (Luke6:38).** We thank God because He is good, His love is tender and continues forever. We give thanks to the God over all gods, the King of kings and the Prince of peace. We give thanks for He is the miracle working Father, the Creator who made the light, heavens, earth, who formed the dry ground, seas, fishes, animals and they were beautiful. He set the sun in the sky to rule over day, moon and stars to rule over the night. We give thanks to the one who made us in His image and likeness. Give thanks to the Father who gave us power and authority to be fruitful, multiply, rule and have dominion over all that He has created. With His mighty power He brought you and I out of the pit. To the God who chose us when we were nothing and call us His own, who rescued us from the power of our enemies and evil one, we give thanks. If we have ten thousand tongues it is not enough to thank God for His provision, protection, security, favours and opportunities. **(See Psalms 107, 116,118, 136,138,139).**

PRAYER OF PRAISE: This is the time to praise God with singing, dancing, clapping, shouting and all kinds of instruments. Praise God for all he has done for you, for open doors that no man can open/shut. Praise the one who makes things happen. When you have done all you can and cannot figure out how to come out of your difficult situation, praise Him. Praise Him with everything you have. This is the time to ignore your ego and praise Him like you have never done before. Praise the "I Am", the beginning and the end, the first and the last, the unsearchable and dependable God. Praise the God who makes a way when there is no way and makes all things possible when it looks impossible.**(Psalms 117, 135,144,145, 146,147,148,150).** Praise Yahweh whether you feel like it or not. Praise Him when you are weak and when you are strong. Praise Him despite your situation. Sing songs like "Even when it hurts, I will yet praise Him" by Hillsong United, "Though I walk through the valley of the shadow of death, I will fear no evil (Tabernacle choir & Psalms 23). Praise Him and declare "Though he slay me, I will yet praise him" **(Job13:15).** Many people have received their breakthrough just by/when praising Him. The bible says He inhabits the praises of His people **(Psalms22:3 KJV).**

Praise is when you forget about yourself and reach out to God. Forget what is going on around you and concentrate only on your Father. I understand it is difficult for some men to dance in public or dance at home when nothing is happening and there is no music. You must remember you are giving praise to the one who knew you before you were born. Shout, laugh, smile, scream or jump if you have to in your Father's presence. Be content in God's presence. When they brought the ark of God to Jerusalem, King David leapt and danced before the Lord. **Then David returned to bless his household. But [his wife] Michal the daughter of Saul came out to meet David and said, "How glorious and distinguished was the king of Israel today, who uncovered himself and stripped [off his kingly robes] in the eyes of his servants' maids like one of the riffraff who shamelessly uncovers himself!" So David said to Michal, "It was before the Lord [that I did this], who chose me above your father and all his house, to appoint me as ruler over Israel, the people of the Lord. Therefore I will celebrate [in pure enjoyment] before the Lord. Yet I will demean myself even more than this, and will be humbled (abased) in my own sight [and yours, as I please], but by the maids whom you mentioned, by them I shall be held in honor." Michal the daughter of**

Saul had no child to the day of her death. (2 Samuel6:20-23 AMP).

Praise is not an obligation but a deserved attention for your Father. I have noticed that the majority of the people in the western world take for granted the abundance of resources available to them compared to some countries where there is none or few resources to go round. Recently, someone sent me a video of a woman who was grateful for all that God has given her: a family of 6 sharing one room. They eat, shower, study, sleep and play in the same room. The joy and the confidence shown in her face when she showed the world her tremendous beautiful room was remarkable. What I am saying is that Yahweh is more than enough for you and you do not know what tomorrow holds but He does. So give Him the highest praise and let heaven rejoice with you. **It is because of the Lord's loving kindnesses that we are not consumed, Because His [tender] compassions never fail. They are new every morning; Great and beyond measure is Your faithfulness (Lamentation3:22-23 AMP**

PRAYER OF WORSHIP: Worship is another way to express ourselves in God's presence. This is the time to acknowledge His power and greatness. Our God is greater, stronger and wants His children to be great and strong. Worship gives you strength you do not think you have or deserve. There is a different response when you offer your worship to the Lord. **I will bless the Lord at all times, His praise shall continually be in my mouth (Psalms34:1).** I will worship you only and I will not worship any other gods. Jacob's act of worship moved God to visit him. He wrestled with God and would not let Him go until He blessed him and his entire generation **(Genesis32:22-32)**. Worship brings the presence of God and caused god dagon to fall flat on his face. God's presence was so heavy on the people of Ashdod that they decided to send the ark of God that they took back to Israel (**1 Samuel 5**). Worship brings blessings; Obed-edom's household was blessed because of the ark of God **(2samuel6:11).** The presence of God is powerful. Do not underestimate what God can do when you worship and invite His presence into your situation. When I watch marvel movies with my boys, I always notice the same pattern between the good and the bad i.e. a man who demands recognition and prestige which only reminds me of satan who was kicked out of heaven because he wanted to be greater than God. There are so many things that want to steal God's worship from us i.e. time, work, careers, power, money, TV shows, Netflix, society, family. Our flesh is always in conflict with the spirit but we have to make a choice who we want to give our worship to, will it be man or God?

PRAYER FOR CONSECRATION: My understanding of this is divided into two parts. Firstly, it is to set ourselves apart for God to do something i.e. if you need a breakthrough on a prolonged issue/ desire or to hear God on a particular issue, for God's direction and guidance. Secondly, to dedicate our life to Christ and allow God to cleanse, purge and purify us. The bible says we should renew our mind daily so that our accuser (devil) will not have anything against us **(Revelation12:10; 1Peter5:8).**

In the Old Testament we see the atonement of sin with animal sacrifices but we do not have to make any sacrifices because our Lord Jesus made the sacrifice once and for all for us when He died on the cross. His body shed for our sins and His blood atone for our sins. Prayer of Consecration is asking God to cleanse us from our sins **(Psalms51:7NIV/NLT/ESV). David said: Create in me a clean heart, O God and renew a right spirit within, cast me not away from thy presence, take not thy Holy Spirit from me and restore unto me the joy of thy salvation and uphold me with thy free spirit (Psalms51: 10-12KJV).** In the Old Testament, the Lord told Moses to consecrate the Priests **(Exodus 29)** and the children of Israel because He was coming down to speak to them **(Exodus19).** My understanding is that where God is, there is no filth, sin or unrighteousness. Remember also when Moses first encountered God, the Lord told him to take off his sandals because he was on a holy ground **(Exodus3:5).** In many instances in the Old Testament, the Lord commanded the children of Israel to consecrate themselves because of their sins **(Exodus 32; 33; 34; 35 and the book of Leviticus).**

PRAYER OF PETITION /SUPPLICATION: This is when we ask God for what we want Him to do for us. The bible says we should cast all our cares on Him for He cares for us **(1Peter 5:7).** The bible promised that when we ask, God will give us the desires of our heart, when we seek Him, we will find Him and when we knock on the door, it will be opened unto us **(Matthew7:7-8)**.We need to realise that God has already provided what we need and He is just waiting for us to activate His promises. God has given you the power to ask. Can you imagine what would have happened to the man Jesus said to **'Get up, pick up your mat and walk' (John 5:8)**, if he refused to respond to the command? His situation would have remained the same despite what God had said. Faith comes by hearing and hearing by the word of God **(Romans 10:17)**. Do not be like the man by the pool who was sick for 38 years but when Jesus asked him if he wanted to get well, he said that when the water bubbled up he had no one to put him into the pool (excuses). Thank God that the Saviour ignores our responses sometimes and just gives us what we want/need **(John5:1-18)**. If the Lord gave you a blank cheque today and asked you to write something in it, what would it be?

After Solomon had completed building God's house and offered so many offerings to the Lord, that same night God appeared to him and asked him: **"What do you want? Ask, and it will be given to you".** Solomon replied by stating how God showed great and faithful love to David his father, and how grateful he was to be made king in his place. Then, He asked God to continue to keep the promise He made to his father (David) and give him wisdom and knowledge to lead His people properly and acknowledged that he could not do it by his own ability. What a powerful request! Solomon must have touched the heart of God for Him to respond and give him the wisdom and knowledge as requested with an additional of things that Solomon did not ask for which were; long life, wealth, fame such as no other king has never had before **(2Chronicle1:7-12).**

PRAYER OF INTERCESSION: This is an action of intervening on behalf of another. We see from time to time in the bible where Paul asked the body of Christ to pray for him **(2Thessalonians3:1. Colossians4:2, Ephesians6:20, Romans 15:30-32),** and when Martha and Mary asked Jesus to pray for their brother Lazarus **(John11).** Prayer of intercession is used to pray on behalf of someone who is sick, not saved, and needs a breakthrough or deliverance. I remember when I first gave my life to Christ, my attitude was to pray for everyone and anyone even though I did not know much about prayer. My sister stood in the gap for me and I believe I should do the same for others. I appreciate the price she paid praying for me so that I could be allowed to go to fellowship and camp meetings and join the choir in our church. As you pray for others, others will pray for you. I like prayer threads where each person in a group praying for each other daily. It is uplifting to know that someone is praying for me. In our generation today we need a platform where we can intercede for one another. The bible says where two or three gather in His name, He is there to give them what they want **(Matthew18:20).**

PRAYER OF AGREEMENT: This is where two or more agree together in praying for someone or for God's intervention. Prayer of agreement can be done in small house groups or big conferences. I remember during Hillsong colour conference years ago, a #MIDDAYBABYMIDDAY prayer was introduced. Attendees set their alarm for 12pm to pray for our world. It was amazing to be part of it and out of that came awesome testimonies of salvation, prosecution of child trafficking offenders in Asia, school girls rescued from Boko Aram kidnappers in Africa and many more. There are many instances in the bible where miracles happened because the body of Christ prayed. Peter was put in prison by Herod to harm him for preaching the gospel but fervent and persistent prayers were made to God on his behalf by the believers. The bounded chains fell off and he was escorted out of prison by the angel **(Acts12).** In the Old Testament, Abraham engaged in a conversation with the Lord that saved his nephew (Lot) from being destroyed with Sodom and Gomorrah **(Genesis 18 and 19)**. Every Tuesday I pray with my prayer partner and we stand in agreement for our five children including our compassion children. We have seen tremendous miracles of protection from danger, answered prayers and many more.

PRAYER OF COMMUNION: Praying using communion is a way of proclaiming what Jesus did for us on the cross into our current situation. Communion is not only for church services alone, it can be done at home as well. You do not need a priest to conduct this for you. When we bring communion into our home we are acknowledging what Jesus did for us and we are welcoming Him into our homes. When we take communion, we are thanking Him for His body that was broken for us and His blood that was shed for us. When we take communion, we are reminding God of the agreement (Covenant) He made with mankind through His son. Also, we are proclaiming Jesus's death and resurrection until He comes (**1Corinthians11:23-34**). We also use communion to declare health, forgiveness of sin and cleansing from all unrighteousness. Communion can be taken daily, as a form of medication and a declaration. It can be taken individually or as a group. Let the Holy Spirit instruct you on what is best for what you are going through. Jesus broke bread and wine with His disciples and the disciples also demonstrated it (**Matthew26-29 Acts2:42**).

I have taken communion daily for a year when I came off hydroxychloroquine (medication for Lupus) and I thank God for His healing power. Communion can be taken before you go for an interview, start a project etc. Whatever way you choose to take communion, you must believe it will work for you. There are so many discussions around what bread or drink to use. My understanding according to the bible is to use unleavened bread and wine. What does that mean? Well, I have used wafers, crackers, matzah, flatbread and grape juice. What matters is our heart and our motive for taking communion. Jesus's entire life was hung on the cross for the crimes He did not commit. So, it is important to make effort when you are preparing for communion. Prepare your heart to receive what He did for you. Consecrate your heart and make sure nothing filthy is found in it.

1 Corinthians 11:27- 29, So then, anyone who eats this bread or drinks this cup of the Lord unworthily is guilty of sinning against the body and blood of the Lord. That is why you should examine yourself before eating the bread and drinking the cup. For if you eat the bread or drink the cup without honoring the body of Christ, you are eating and drinking God's judgment upon yourself.

There are different scriptures to use for communion: **Matthew 26:29, Mark14:22-25 Luke22:7-22, John6; 1Corinthians11:23-26, Ephesians 1-3**

PRAYER AND CONFESSION

Lord, I thank You that I can talk to you in so many ways

I thank God for His blessings and promises that never fail

I am not ashamed to lift up my hands to worship God

I will not shy away to dance, sing and express myself in God's presence

I am a prayer warrior and I will pray for myself and those around me.

I will always remember the sacrifice Jesus paid on my behalf and celebrate my freedom

I will give thanks at all times. In good and bad time, in the time of plenty and the time of famine **(Philippians4:11-13)**

I will not be ungrateful, moan or complain when I have not received my promise. I will be content in all seasons of my life and be thankful

May my offering of praise, worship and thanksgiving be received by Heaven. I will not be silent but I will always worship my Lord.

Jesus did not just teach on prayer, he demonstrated prayer. The evidence of prayer will be seen in my life and everything that pertains to me

My prayer life will encourage and challenge others to pray

I receive boldness to pray effectively and directly for any situation

I will use prayer to fight the battle that comes my way

I pray for discernment to know what and how to pray for others

I pray that the words that I have proclaimed over my life, will not return back to Yahweh void but they will accomplish what I desire and achieve their purpose. **(Isaiah55:11)**

Cleanse me, wash me with the blood of Jesus. Let the sound of joy and gladness not cease from my mouth **(Psalms51:7-8)**

Create in me a pure heart, O God, and renew a steadfast spirit within me. Do not cast me from your presence or take your Holy Spirit from me. Restore to me the joy of your salvation and grant me a willing spirit to sustain me (**Psalms51:10-12)**

RESPONSE TO PRAYER

God responds to prayers, He is alive and He speaks to His children in different ways i.e. the bible, dreams, visions, spiritual gifts. When we pray to God, we are not praying to a dead god or images that cannot talk. Why do the nations say, **"Where is their God?" Our God is in heaven; he does whatever pleases him. But their idols are silver and gold, made by human hands. They have mouths, but cannot speak, eyes, but cannot see. They have ears, but cannot hear, noses, but cannot smell. They have hands, but cannot feel, feet, but cannot walk, nor can they utter a sound with their throats. Those who make them will be like them, and so will all who trust in them (Psalms115:2-8).** When you pray you should expect that God will hear your prayers and give you the desires of your heart. Some prayers are answered instantly and I love that, but it does not often happen to me. However, I have an assurance that when I pray, the Lord has heard me because He says if I call upon His name over anything, He will do it **(John14:14).**

Whenever I engage in a conversation with someone, I expect them to respond back to me whether through words or actions. I work with people with learning disabilities (which means they might be non- verbal in their communication), even then I still expect them to nod their head or give me a gesture to establish that they have understood what I am saying. At work we used to have two black cats (sisters), I would talk to them as I would to humans, cared for them by giving them water and food and in return they brought me a present to show their gratitude which I did not appreciate or like because it was either a dead or live mouse. It was as if they knew when I will be on shift and waited at the front door for me. How much more for the God who created all things, who knows what we want and He will do it for us at the appointed time? He said, He will not withhold good things from those who walk uprightly with Him **(Psalms84:11 KJV).**

However, there are some prayers that are delayed for different reasons, not because of what we have done or not done but the fact that our Father knows what we need at the right time. **Ecclesiastes 3 explains that there is time for everything and a season for every activity on earth. So, when we pray we must believe that God is able to do what we asked and grant our requests at the right time**. Delays are definitely not a denial, if He promised, He will bring it to pass. His promises never fail and He is a promise keeping God. The only problem with us humans is that we give up too soon or assume He is not going to do it because He did not do it at the time we wanted Him to do it for us. This reminds me of a story in Daniel 10: **Suddenly, a hand touched me, which made me tremble on my knees and on the palms of my hands. And he said to me, "O Daniel, man greatly beloved, understand the words that I speak to you, and stand upright, for I have now been sent to you." While he was speaking this word to me, I stood trembling. Then he said to me, "Do not fear, Daniel, for from the first day that you set your heart to understand, and to humble yourself before your God, your words were heard; and I have come because of your words. But the prince of the kingdom of Persia withstood me twenty-one** days; and behold, Michael, one of the chief princes, came to help me, for I had been left alone there with the kings of Persia. Now I have come to make you understand what will happen to your people in the latter days, for the vision refers to many days yet to come." (Verse 10-15NKJV)

The reason some prayers are delayed may be our thoughts/ perceptions/ confessions. Do you believe in what you are asking from God? Do you know the authority you have to ask in boldness? Do you know that there is power in the name of Jesus to do what you want Him to do for you? Is your heart right about what you are asking from the Lord? When the angel of the Lord appeared to Gideon he was in a place where he had lost hope and did not believe in miracles any longer. He had so many questions for God which the He answered patiently **(Judges6:11-16). In Verves 17-22 we saw his conversation with the angel of the Lord: Gideon replied, "If now I have found favor in your eyes, give me a sign that it is really you talking to me. Please do not go away until I come back and bring my offering and set it before you." And the Lord said, "I will wait until you return." Gideon went inside, prepared a young goat, and from an ephah of flour he made bread without yeast. Putting the meat in a basket and its broth in a pot, he brought them out and offered them to him under the oak. The angel of God said to him, "Take the meat and the unleavened bread, place them on this rock, and pour out the broth." And Gideon did so. Then the angel of the Lord touched the meat and the unleavened bread with the tip of the staff that was in his hand. Fire flared**

from the rock, consuming the meat and the bread. And the angel of the Lord disappeared. When Gideon realized that it was the angel of the Lord, he exclaimed, "Alas, Sovereign Lord! I have seen the angel of the Lord face to face!"

Waiting might not be a pleasant experience as everything looks the same, we feel stuck, we cannot see a way out and on top of it we cannot hear God. I have heard many Christians say that they cannot hear God speak to them in a season of their life. Perhaps they need to check their relationship with God? Find out how the Lord speaks to you, because God speak to us differently. Are you willing and obedient to do what He tells you to do? Can you recognise the voice of God and the voice of the devil **(John 15)?** There is a saying that practice makes perfect. I am not saying we have to be perfect before God but the more we spend time with Him the more we get to know Him and how He operates in our life, He is a relational God. Isaiah 55 tells us that God's thoughts and ways are not like human beings, once He says something, it will not return void without accomplishing it **(verse8-11). Trust that God will give you your miracle in due season. The bible says, "weeping may endure for a night but joy comes in the morning" (Psalms30:5NKJV).** When our miracle finally arrives, it will be like what the Israelites described in **Psalms126: When the Lord brought back the captivity of Zion, We were like those who dream. Then our mouth was filled with laughter, And our tongue with singing. Then they said among the nations, "The Lord has done great things for**

them." The Lord has done great things for us, And we are glad (verse1-3NKJV).

If you find yourself in a season of waiting i.e. waiting for promotion, a project, opportunities, a career or business, no matter the nature of the waiting, don't give up. Believe me when I say He will answer, I am a witness. I was diagnosed with Lupus in 2013, I know I am healed because my Father promised me. I have seen tremendous recovery take place in my body and I believe there is yet more healing to come. Am I healed? Yes. Do I no longer have health issues? No. There are things that came with the diagnosis or have been part of my life that the Holy Spirit is just revealing to me that I am working on, as I get closer to Him. What I am saying is that you cannot give up or think God is not hearing you. **Have you not known? Have you not heard? The everlasting God, the Lord, the Creator of the ends of the earth, neither faints nor is weary. His understanding is unsearchable. He gives power to the weak, and to those who have no might He increases strength. Even the youths shall faint and be weary, And the young men shall utterly fall, But those who wait on the Lord Shall renew their strength; They shall mount up with wings like eagles, They shall run and not be weary, They shall walk and not faint.(Isaiah 40:28-31)** What should I do while waiting on God to do something for me? Thank and praise Him for the manifestation and surround yourself with His promises regarding the matter. This is the time to thank Him for what He has said to you personally through His word, dreams, word of knowledge. However, what you do not want to do while waiting is to complain. This only delays your breakthrough as we see in the story of the Israelites when they left Egypt. The journey that was meant to take 11 days took 40 years.

Many times in my life I have mistaken what God was saying to mean something else. I did not seek His face to get more understanding of what He was saying which only prolonged answers to my prayers or received no answers at all. David always inquired of the Lord before he went to war, even when his best friend (Jonathan) did not believe that his dad (Saul) wanted to harm David. David already knew his life was in danger with Saul **(1Samuel20).** Learn to recognise how God speaks to you. I have known the Lord for a while now but I must confess I am just realising how God speaks to me. The way you interpret what people say to you is the same way God speaks to you. For instance, I am pictorial when it comes to the way I process things. True life stories and practical things resonate with me more than theory. God responds to us the way we will understand. King Saul was tired of waiting for the time set by Samuel that he decided to offer burnt offerings that was meant to be done by Samuel the priest and as soon as he made the offering Samuel came and it was too late to reverse what he had done: **"What have you done?" asked Samuel. Saul replied, "When I saw that the men were scattering, and that you did not come at the set time, and that the Philistines were assembling at Mikmash, I thought, 'Now the Philistines will come down against me at Gilgal, and I have not sought the Lord's favor.' So I felt compelled to offer the burnt offering." "You have done a foolish thing," Samuel said. "You have not kept the**

command the Lord your God gave you; if you had, he would have established your kingdom over Israel for all time. But now your kingdom will not endure; the Lord has sought out a man after his own heart and appointed him ruler of his people, because you have not kept the Lord's command." (1Samuel13:11-14). Obedience is better than sacrifice and faith comes by hearing the word of God and receiving it. The bible says: **Faith is the substance of things hoped for, the evidence of things not seen. (Hebrew11:1)** You have to believe you have received your blessings even before you see the manifestation. **Jesus said to Thomas, blessed are those who believe in Him without seeing Him (John20:29).**

Faith might be the key to your unanswered prayers. Sometimes our situation might feel like we are sinking but if we call on Jesus like Peter did, He will rescue us. He is the author and the finisher of our faith, He will carry our burden and open doors that seem closed for years. A moment in His presence might just be what God needs to carry out your requests. Thank Him and worship His name in every season of life. Most of the promises God gives requires us to do something before we can receive the promise. In **Deuteronomy 11,** God mentioned fifteen things we have to do in order to receive what He has promised; Love God, Listen carefully, Pay attention, Do what is right in God's eyes, Seek God, Observe, Obey, Hold fast, Be Faithful, Walk in obedience, Plant the word in our heart, Be careful of following other gods, Teach your children, Write down and Carefully observe the word of God. **(See other scriptures John 14:27;**

Leviticus 26:3 4; John15:4; Joshua 1:9; Hebrews 10:34-36; Isaiah 54:2-5).

Lack of faith is one of the reasons our prayers do not get answered. Having done all to do, stand right! It is not as simple as it sounds. Going through my waiting period, I have heard my brothers and sisters say to me I lack faith or do not have enough faith. Is that right for them to say that to me knowing I was going through a difficult time? Maybe or maybe not but it surely gave me the kick I needed to press forward to know God more for myself and believe God for my miracles. All Jesus requires from us is little faith, right! **(Luke17:6).** No matter how small or big our request is, the Lord knows and He will grant it to us for His name to be glorified. There was a lot against the crippled man who was brought to Jesus by his four friends through the ceiling but their faith got Jesus's attention and healed him **(Mark 2:1-5NKJV). The bible told us that a doubter and people who are unstable in their ways will not receive anything from God (James1:5-8).** Faith is what unlocks a miracle not our emotions or how eloquent we sound in the presence of God. Jesus was amazed by a centurion who came to Him to heal his servant: When Jesus heard it, He marvelled, and said to those who followed, **"Assuredly, I say to you, I have not found such great faith, not even in Israel! (Matthew 8:10NKJV)**

After you have done all you can and there is no breakthrough, leave it to God. The bible says having done all, stand firm **(Ephesians6:13).**There are some things for everyone and some things that are just uniquely for you and for God to be glorified in your life.

When Mary and Martha sent a message to Jesus that their brother was ill, Jesus did not go straightaway. He waited four days when Joseph was already buried. Why? For His Father to be glorified. The miracle God gives us, even though it is ours, it is also for others to know that there is a God in heaven who answers prayer. Not everyone is going to get married or divorced. Not everyone will have biological children but will have the opportunity to adopt or foster children. There is time for everything. The bible tells us there are different seasons under heaven. So, if you are praying for something and cannot see a result yet, go back to your Father and let Him reveal to you what you cannot see with your physical eyes. It took Gehazi seven times to see the cloud that Elisha was telling him about **(1Kings18:43-44).** In another instance, Elisha had to pray to God for his servant so that he could see the horses and chariots that were for them to surf the problems ahead of them **(2Kings6:17-20).** Most of the battles we face require us to be closer to God in order for us to see what is against us and what is for us.

The time of waiting should be spent wisely. It is not the time to devise plan B or put matters into our hands or do things without proper instructions from the master-God. Majority of things we ask for and we do not get are not meant for us to have them in the first place. Do not live your life based on the way the world does, or how culture/religion wants you to. You may think you are helping God by doing things your way but in reality you are adding more problems to the situation. We see this in the life of Abram and Sarai. Sarai had given up that God could give them a child because she believed they had gone past the age of bearing children **(Genesis18)**. Did God tell them that or it was their imagination running wild on them? The decision they both made by having Ismael is probably what is causing problems in the Middle East today. You might not think much of the choices you are making today but the consequences of making a wrong decision may affect generations to come. So think about what you are asking God. The Lord does not need our help to do what He has already promised to do in our life. If you knew that your car needed petrol, why would you take it to a mechanic to check what was wrong with it? If you knew that your prayer has been answered you will not worry too much as to when God will do what you have been asking Him to do for you. He who has promised is faithful and He will fulfil His promise to you.

So, relax the answer is on the way.

PRAYER AND CONFESSION

Heavenly Father, I am thankful I can call on You and You will answer me. I hereby, place my request before You **(1Peter5:7)**. Tell God your requests……..

I thank God for all that He has done, what He is doing and what He will yet do in my life.

I ask for forgiveness for many times I have doubted God's ability to perform wonders in my life. I have believed the lies of the enemy over Your promises, I am sorry. Forgive me for the times I have complained when I did not see what I have asked for.

Help me to be content with Your promises and to believe that You are able to do exceedingly and abundantly more than I can ask or dream **(Philippians 4:11-13)**.

Lord, I believe there is no mountain You cannot move, no valley You cannot make low, no goliath that You cannot defeat and no burdens You cannot remove. For there is nothing too difficult or impossible for You **(Mark 10:27)**.

When my faith is weak, take me to the rock that is higher than me. Increase my strength the all sufficient God. Stir up my faith when it crumbles. Give me patience in times of waiting, Let me not look at what I cannot do but what You can do. My desire is to trust in God not lean on my understanding and to acknowledge God in all my ways and I know He will direct my path **(Proverbs3:5-7)**.

May I not be jealous/envious of other people God has blessed instead celebrate with them and believe that the God who did it for them will surely do it for me.

I will obey God's commands and keep His decrees

I am thankful for my miracle, promotion that is on the way.

THE ARMOUR OF GOD

The armour of God is a weapon for believers to fight the battle of life and protect themselves from whatever plan the enemy has in mind. On the 21st of April 2020, I came across **Ephesians 6** like I have never seen before and the revelation that the Holy Spirit gave me is something I cannot keep to myself, I have to share it with you. I have not studied "The armour of God" in details or understood what it meant prior to that day. I am sure that there are plenty of books and teachings out there on the subject.

During the Covid19 pandemic so many people were ill or died. There was fear, confusion, financial crisis, lockdown, isolation, specialists' exhaustion and the world had been thrown into a limbo. Indeed the world needs the whole Armour of God. I was so overwhelmed by news of parents dying and leaving young children behind as well as young people dying and leaving the parents. Prayer requests from those asking God to spare the grandad as grandma just died, prayer for loved ones on the verge of death. I cried to God for mercy. It was in the midst of this thought that my sister called me and told me about her previous day at work (she works in the hospital). I tried not to show my emotions as she talked and then she said, "I prayed to Yahweh not to take this 89year old man as the wife just died two days ago. I prayed there will be no death on my ward and God honoured my prayer and no one died on that day". Apparently, four people died on the same ward a day before when she was not on shift. That evening, I was encouraged by another story of a lady who needed surgery and the children of God prayed and the surgery went well. This lifted up my spirit to trust God more and know that even when I do not see or feel it, God is working.

So, it is not a surprise that my eye was drawn to verse 10 of Ephesians 6 which encouraged me to "be strong in the Lord and in his mighty power". My faith was strengthened and I knew I can face another day by His Grace. I realised I do not have to do anything alone or with my strength, God is with me. To Him be the glory. How can I be strong in the Lord and His mighty power? **Ephesians 6:10-17NIV says finally, be strong in the Lord and in his mighty power. Put on the full armor of God, so that you can take your stand against the devil's schemes. For our struggle is not against flesh and blood, but against the rulers, against the authorities, against the powers of this dark world and against the spiritual forces of evil in the heavenly realms. Therefore put on the full armor of God, so that when the day of evil comes, you may be able to stand your ground, and after you have done everything, to stand. Stand firm then, with the belt of truth buckled around your waist, with the breastplate of righteousness in place, and with your feet fitted with the readiness that comes from the gospel of peace. In addition to all this, take up the shield of faith, with which you can extinguish all the flaming arrows of the evil one. Take the helmet of salvation and the sword of the Spirit, which is the word of God.**

Wow! Just the medicine the doctor prescribed and I surely need the full armour of God in my life.

Straightaway, I googled the meaning of armour and this is what I got: strong covering that protect something, especially the body. Kind of what the soldiers, army or police wear to protect them from getting killed. A soldier cannot go to war without a weapon and protective gear just like a believer cannot go to battle without putting on the full armour of God. No amount of protection can prepare you for what you will face in the battle. It is not about our power but God's mighty power. An army that goes to battle would not know whether they will return home or not but they are confident in the training they have received. I have just finished watching a series of "Our girls" on Netflix, and as I watched the episodes, I realised you cannot prepare enough for the battle ahead of you. Only God can guide and direct your path. So, why then do believers assume going to battle will be easy and that we know everything that we needed to know about the battle? The battle belongs to the Lord. With every battle we face comes strength from above to overcome and the strength can only come when believers spend time in God's presence. **John 16:33 "I have told you these things, so that in me ye may have peace. In the world you will have trouble. But take heart! I have overcome the world". Also, in 1 Corinthians10:13NKJV, it says, "No temptation has overtaken you except such as is common to man; but God is faithful, who will not allow you to be tempted beyond what you able, but with the temptation will also make way of escape, that you may be able to bear It".**

The full armour of God is a strong covering that protects those who believe in God. **Who is your**

covering? Your strength that may fail you, let you down or abandon you when you need it most? Let your strength come from the one who makes heaven and earth. The one that made you in His image and breathe life into you. **Proverbs 3: 5&6 says, "Trust in the Lord with all your heart and lean not on your own understanding; in all your ways submit to him, and he will make your paths straight"**

What is the aim of an armour? To protect us from the schemes of the devil. The serpent or the devil or the enemy, whichever way you prefer to call him, has an agenda; to steal, kill and destroy **(John 10:10a).**The serpent was described as being more subtle and crafty than any living creature which the Lord God had made **(Genesis 3:1a AMPC).**

The following are some of my past experiences with the crafty creature: He will twist God's command to suit his own agenda. He will compromise God's instructions. He will make us to question God's authority over our lives. He will make us to undermine God and elevate our self. He will tell us lies so we can make wrong decisions. He will make us to believe his lies over God's promises .He will make us desire him more than God .His ultimate goal is to turn us away from God. He will use his cunning ways to distract us from the truth and magnifies problems. He will make us fearful over things that might or might not happen. He is jealous that the man created after him was given dominion over him and He will deceive us. He will make you think your plan is better than God's plan, or you are better than God or you do not need God and many more lies. I am not glorifying him, I am just letting you know he is not your friend. He is your enemy and you cannot afford to toil with him. He is a fraud, schemer, a disgrace and a disappointment of God's creatures. Always remember he was kicked out of heaven, hell is his home now and will not stop at nothing to bring more people to join him there. **1Peter5:8 says he roams around to and fro looking for whom to devour. Our job in this matter is to submit to God, resist the devil and the devil will flee from us (James4:8).** Do not give him a place in your life. Do not welcome, encourage or entertain him in any way. You should not be afraid of him either, he should be afraid of you because you carry Yahweh's power and authority. **Psalms 91:13 NKJV says "You shall tread upon the lion and the cobra, the young lion and the serpent you shall trample underfoot. The second part of John 10:10b tell us that Jesus came that we will have life in full.** If you do not know this God that I am talking about and you want to know Him, it is simple. All you have to do is acknowledge that He is Lord. Ask him to forgive you of your sins and invite Him to come into your life in Jesus's name. Congratulations! If you made the decision to follow Jesus, you are now a candidate and citizen of heaven. You have not missed out, all you have to do is to plug into His teaching which we are looking at right now

Why do we need to put on the armour of God?

*to stand against the devil's schemes

*to help with our struggles against rulers, authorities, power of dark and evil world and spiritual forces in heaven *to be able to stand our ground in the days of evil

*to stand firm

Now let us look at each armour of God.

Belt of truth buckled round our waist: A belt holds things together i.e. trousers, skirts, dresses. It is amazing that the bible used the 'belt' to illustrate the truth in order for believers to understand the truth of God that we know must be worn at all times. The bible says you shall know the truth and the truth will set you free **(John8:32).** You cannot lose your grip on the truth of God's word. Meditate, study, write this truth on the tablet of your heart **(Proverbs3:3).** It is not enough to know the truth, you need to practice what it says. The word of God is not just a memory verse, we need to follow the principles and obey the instructions. Without this truth we cannot stand against the devil's devices. No matter how intelligent you are, you cannot outrun the devil by your power alone, you need God's power. If you don't know what the truth is, you will not know the difference when you are told lies. And we know that the devil is the father of lies. Jesus said, He is the way, the truth and the life. No one comes to the Father except through Him **(John 14:6).** Jesus also said, the truth you know will set you free **(John 8:31-32).** The truth is what keeps the enemy away from us. It is what differentiates believers from those who do not believe. There is no small lie or white lie, a lie is a lie. Stay away from lies, you cannot serve two masters. You have to choose one that will not get you into trouble. You say well, I do get away with lies and I have never been caught. There is a saying in my language, "Every day is for the thief and one day is for the owner". In other words, one day your bad behaviour will catch up with you. I have heard colleagues say that 'he called himself/herself a Christian and he/she lies a lot'. This is not a testimony that brings praise to our Father."

To walk our journey of faith we have to put on the belt of truth and buckle it round our waist everywhere we go. Do not leave home without it. Do not leave your house without talking to your Father and reading His truth. In these days where we have mobile phones, none of us will dare to leave home without our phone or not charge it. We even carry a power bank to charge our phone on the go, so we never run out of battery. In the west, we take for granted the luxury of having internet/ Wi-Fi whenever we want and we have no excuse to not reading as many versions of the bible as we want. I am really grateful for my home broadband during 2020 lockdown as life was quite not the same where my mother lives. She is 85years old and had been told to shield but things were not going so well. There was no constant power for electricity making it impossible to listen or watch a Sunday service or charge her phone. In some parts of the world, many do not even have a bible or freedom to even meet to share the gospel. War has turned a whole nation into ruins and even in the midst of the wreckage many still show how grateful they are to the King of Kings and the Lord of Lords. Why not invest time to study the truth so that you are able to stand your ground in the days of evil. Take truth everywhere you go.

Breastplate of Righteousness: Breastplate is a piece of armour covering the chest. The dictionary meaning of breastplate or chest plate is a device worn over the torso to protect it from injury. What is a torso? A torso is the trunk of the human body. I am thinking about the bulletproof vests police officers wear to protect them against any harm. Or safety vests that horse riders wear to protect the torso if they fall. Now that we have established what breastplate is, let's look at righteousness. Righteousness is the quality of being morally right or justifiable according to the dictionary. But what does the word 'moral' mean? Holding or manifesting high principles for proper conduct. In other words, there is a high standard of right standing that the Lord requires of believers to maintain at all times which cannot be achieved by our human strength. **Thus says the Lord, "Let not a wise man boast of his wisdom, and let not the mighty man boast of his might, let not a rich man boast of his riches; but let him who boasts boast of this, that he understands and knows Me, that I am the Lord who exercises lovingkindness, justice and righteousness on earth; for I delight in these things," declares the Lord. (Jeremiah 9:23-24).**The bible says the Lord is righteous and He loves righteousness **(Psalms11:7).**

As believers we do not have to be afraid of the devil because the Lord will strengthen us, help us and uphold us with His righteous right hand **(Isaiah 41:10).** We ought to put on the Breastplate of righteousness to protect us from the devices of the devil, live a life based on Godly principles so that the enemy cannot point a finger at us. You won't get it right most of the time but your heart to do what is right is your Father's delight. We are not perfect, only God is perfect. Protect your body, soul and spirit. How?

Body: Adopt a healthy lifestyle by exercising regularly, eating and drinking food that will nourish and strengthen our body rather than junk.

Soul: Guard your heart with the word of God. Guard what you listen to, what you watch, the type of friends you have and the people who feed into your life.
Finally, brothers and sisters, whatever is true, whatever is noble, whatever is right, whatever is pure, whatever is lovely, whatever is admirable—if anything is excellent or praiseworthy—think about such things. Whatever you have learned or received or heard from me, or seen in me—put it into practice. And the God of peace will be with you. Philippians 4:8-9.

Spirit: Keep your spirit clean. Do not grieve the Holy Spirit with your works of the flesh. The paragraph below explains the 'works of the flesh'.

Galatians5:19-25 says, Now the works of the flesh are manifest, which are these; Adultery, fornication, uncleanness, lasciviousness, Idolatry, witchcraft, hatred, variance, emulations, wrath, strife, sedition, heresies, Envy, murder, drunkenness, revelling, and such like: of the which I tell you before, as I have also told you in time past, that they which do such things shall not inherit the kingdom of God. But the fruit of the Spirit is love, joy, peace, longsuffering, gentleness, goodness, faith, Meekness,

temperance: against such there is no law. And they that are Christ's have crucified the flesh with the affections and lusts. If we live in the Spirit, let us also walk in the Spirit.

Make **Psalms 51:10-12** your daily prayer to abstain yourself from immorality and any sinful nature. **Create in me a pure heart, O God, and renew a steadfast spirit within me. Do not cast me from your presence or take your Holy Spirit from me. Restore to me the joy of your salvation and grant me a willing spirit, to sustain me.** Live a life that honours God. Feed your spirit with the word of God. Cultivate a lifestyle that covers your body, soul and spirit and walk in His ways. Put on the breastplate of righteousness to help with your struggles against rulers, authorities, powers of the dark and evil world and spiritual forces in heaven.

Feet: The word of God is a lamp to our feet and light to our path **(Psalm119:105).** The Lord protects us from bashing our feet against the stone **(Luke4:11).** I have heard people say they "go wherever their feet take them". To me that is kind of lack of direction and you are not in control. The bible says people perish for lack of vision. Let your feet be controlled by your Father who is in heaven. The heart of our Father is that none should perish but everyone should enter the kingdom of heaven. Our assignment as ambassadors is to make sure that the heart of the Father is established on earth. As it is in Heaven so let it be done on earth. If we want to follow Christ, we need to be ready at all times to follow His commands and keep

His decrees. Then he said to them all: **"Whoever wants to be my disciple must deny themselves and take up their cross daily and follow me. (Luke 9:23).**

This does not imply that you forget about your life, friends and family. This simply means follow the Lord with all your heart, mind, thoughts and influence the people around you with the image and likeness of your Father. We are called to go into the world and preach the gospel of peace. In the world where peace looks unachievable, there is turmoil all around us, there is knife crime news every day, injustice and hatred have plummeted in our society, we need to bring hope to the world that cannot see hope. The bible says we are the light and the salt of the world. We are the ones to proclaim the good news to the world. I rejoice whenever people make a decision to follow Jesus and I know heaven is excited too. But there are still billions of people around us who do not yet know Christ. Why not start telling the people closer to you (family, friends, neighbour, colleague, employer, lecturer including those who despise you and ridicule you) about Christ? Jesus gave his disciples power and authority to tell people about the kingdom of God, drive out all demons and heal the sick. He told them: **"Take nothing for the journey—no staff, no bag, no bread, no money, no extra shirt. Whatever house you enter, stay there until you leave that town. If people do not welcome you, leave their town and shake the dust off your feet as a testimony against them (Luke 9:1-5)".** We have been given the same power and authority and all we need now is to go and do that which has been commission into our hands. When you wake up in the morning, think about your loved ones who will miss heaven if death came crawling at their door today. I am not here to scare you but to bring to reality that the people you do life with on a daily basis might not make it if Jesus appears today. Do your part and leave the rest to the Holy Spirit who will quicken their mortal body.

I hear people say 'but I do not know how to tell my friend about God because I do not want anything to affect our friendship'. When the hearts of the Israelites hardened and would not listen or follow the command of the Lord, the word of the Lord came to Ezekiel: **"Son of man, I have made you a watchman for the people of Israel; so hear the word I speak and give them warning from me. When I say to a wicked person, 'You will surely die,' and you do not warn them or speak out to dissuade them from their evil ways in order to save their life, that wicked person will die for their sin, and I will hold you accountable for their blood. But if you do warn the wicked person and they do not turn from their wickedness or from their evil ways, they will die for their sin; but you will have saved yourself"(Ezekiel 3:16-19).** So therefore, I would rather say what is in the heart of my Father and save my friends from hell. I would rather reverence God than fear men. If you do not know how to witness to your friends, ask the Holy Spirit and remember when you seek to do what is in the heart of your Father, He will bless you.

We are different in the way we communicate with one another. Why not start today because someone has to start the conversation, let that conversation be the one that leads to eternity. I struggle to witness to total strangers and sometimes I get stuck on how to start the conversation but I have realised that when I commit it to Yahweh and allow Him to lead the conversation, miracles always happen. Not everyone will be interested or want to listen but you do not want to miss those who are itching to know the truth about your Father. Many are so convinced that they know Him but they do not. They have only heard about Him not experienced Him. It is impossible for me to say I know my readers when I have not met them or had a conversation with them. **Romans 10:13-15** explains to us how important it is to do our part in telling others about Jesus: **For, "Everyone who calls on the name of the Lord will be saved." How, then, can they call on the one they have not believed in? And how can they believe in the one of whom they have not heard? And how can they hear without someone preaching to them? And how can anyone preach unless they are sent? As it is written: "How beautiful are the feet of those who bring good news!"** Let your feet be fitted with the readiness that comes from the gospel of peace. **Read Matthew 10 and check the recommended books page to help get you started.**

SHIELD OF FAITH: When I looked up the meaning of shield, this is what came up: a broad piece of metal or another suitable material, held by straps or a handle attached on one side, used as a protection against blows or missiles. Another definition of shield is, a person or a thing providing protection from danger, risk, or unpleasant experience. The Lord is our strength and shield **(Psalm28:7). Psalms33.20 says: Our soul waits for the Lord; He is our help and our shield. Psalms89:18 says: For our shield belongs to the Lord, our king to the Holy One.** The Lord will shield us from any danger. Now that we have an idea of what a shield is, what is faith? The dictionary definition of faith is to completely trust or have confidence in someone or something. As believers, we need to completely trust God. We cannot go to battle without the shield of faith. Faith is the vessel that puts our prayers into action. The bible says without faith it is impossible to please God, for whoever comes to Him must believe that He exists and He is the rewarder of those who sincerely seek him **(Hebrew11:6).** During the Covid19 pandemic, shielding was a word used to categorise people who were at a high risk of being affected by the virus and needed to stay at home to protect themselves and their family. But we know the one who owns the universe will shield us from any pestilence or diseases **(Psalm91:4-8).**

Our prayers, activated by faith will bring manifestation in our life. **Hebrews11:1 ESV** tells us that **faith is the assurance of things hoped for and conviction of things not seen.** In other words, when I pray I need to believe that I have the answer even before I see it. When athletics stand on the track, the only thing they think about is winning a gold, bronze or silver medal. None of them in their right mind wish to fail. So, when things are not going as planned or we are overwhelmed by what is going on around us, let us put our trust in our Father. He is aware of the situation and He is working it out for our good. Jesus told his disciples in **Matthew17:20**, the kind of faith we need to have: **"if you have faith as small as a mustard seed, you can say to this mountain, 'Move from here to there,' and it will move. Nothing will be impossible for you."** In other words, there is no small faith, faith is faith in the eyes of God. It is either you have faith or you don't.

At the beginning of the lockdown, I found myself in a dilemma as to whether to go to work or take the government advice to stay home due to my health. I battled with this for weeks and I remember asking the Lord what I should do. He told me to trust Him and not to put my trust in my employer. After explaining the situation to my employer, he told me he was not going to pay me because I am a bank staff. So I went back to the Lord and He told me to trust Him and not lean on my own understanding. The following Tuesday, a friend of mine paid £100 into my account (she said the Lord told her to give me the money). Saturday of the same week, my connect group gave me £400 (unknown to me that they were contributing). Two weeks after the conversation with my employer, he decided to pay half of my wages because 2 ladies at head office fought for me to get paid (unknown to me). God was working behind the scene and making all things work for my good. I had to trust that God will look after my needs. I did not know how but I trusted in His word even when I was worried subconsciously, He honoured my little faith. My praise goes to Him. If you find yourself in a season where your faith is weak, cry to God for a booster. Read every scripture you can find on faith and the circumstances you are going through to ignite your faith and make the situation work for your good. **Daily, put on the Shield of faith in order to extinguish all the flaming arrows of the evil one.**

HELMET OF SALVATION: Take the helmet of salvation and the sword of the Spirit, which is the word of God. A helmet is what you wear on your head for protection. Cyclists wear it to protect them in case of accidents. People who suffer from epilepsy also wear it to protect themselves from getting hurt if they fall. My understanding of this armour is to protect our salvation. Do not neglect God's teachings and instructions just because you are now born again. **The bible says, to continue to work out our salvation with fear and trembling (Philippians2:12b).** David said, **"Restore unto me the joy of your salvation" when Prophet Nathan confronted him of the sin he committed (Psalms51:12).** The bible says let who stand take heed so that he will not fall **(1 Corinthians10:12).** Many times in the bible, Jesus, the apostle and the prophet warned us to be alert, vigilant and stand firm **(Matthew26:41;Deuteronomy4:9; 1Peter5:8).** Our Salvation is precious to God and that is why **Psalms91:16** says: **For those who call upon the Lord will be satisfy with long life and He will show them His salvation.** Our salvation is what guaranteed our eternal life. We need to wear it everywhere we go and people around us need to see that we are believers. There is no point telling people we believe in Jesus and our character and behaviour does not reflect who we are claiming to believe. There was a story in Acts 19 that came to my mind: **some Jews who went around driving out evil spirits tried to invoke the name of the Lord Jesus over those who were demon-possessed. They would say, "In the name of the Jesus whom Paul preaches, I command you to come out." Seven sons of Sceva, a Jewish chief priest, were doing this. One day the evil spirit answered them, "Jesus I know, and Paul I know about, but who are you?" Then the man who had the evil spirit jumped on them and overpowered them all. He gave them such a beating that they ran out of the house naked and bleeding (Acts19:13-16).** The Lord knows those who are His and the devil knows it as well. So, it is important to protect ourselves by staying close to God, spend time to know Him and honour Him with our life.

PRAYER AND CONFESSION

I thank God for the revelation that there is an enemy and we have the power and might to stand against the devices of the evil one.

I thank the Lord for His protection

I receive the truth of God's Word

I remain in right standing with God

I am ready to tell others about God

I put on the helmet of salvation which is the word of God

I receive the shield of faith

God is strong and He wants me to be strong. I will win the battle of life through Jesus who gives me strength **(Ephesians6:10-12 MSG)**

I overcome the schemes of the devil by the blood of Jesus

I believe I have victory over everything that confronts me

I am brave, strong and courageous to face my fears and the fears of the future

I put on the full armour of God and receive freedom from everything that is standing in my way of progress, purpose, success, destiny, joy and peace

I have the tools to fight my enemies and I will use them for God's glory

I heed the instruction and the counsel of Yahweh. I will not depart from it

I will not go out of my house without putting the whole armour of God

I will not deliberately put myself in danger and give the enemy room to ride over my head

I understand the devil is not my friend, so therefore I will not entertain him in anyway. I will not stroke the enemy of my soul on the head or make him my pet but I will kill the enemy who wants to steal, kill and destroy me by the fire of the Holy Ghost.

The weapons we fight with are not the weapons of the world. On the contrary, they have divine power to demolish strongholds. We demolish arguments and every pretension that sets itself up against the knowledge of God, and we take captive every thought to make it obedient to Christ. And we will be ready to punish every act of disobedience, once your obedience is complete (2Chorinthians10:4-6). I understand I am fighting the enemy of my soul and the weapon God has given me which is the armour of God will be used for His glory. I will use the armour to cast down imaginations and every high things that want to exalt itself against the knowledge of God, bringing into captivity every thought to the obedience of Christ.

"Be prepared. You're up against far more than you can handle on your own. Take all the help you can get, every weapon God has issued, so that when it's all over you'll still be on your feet. Truth, righteousness, peace, faith, and salvation are more than words. Learn how to apply them. You'll need them throughout your life. God's word is an indispensable weapon. In the same way, prayer is essential in this ongoing warfare. Pray hard and long. Pray for your brothers and sisters. Keep your eyes open. Keep each other's spirits up so that no one falls behind or drops out" (Ephesians6:13-18 MSG)

SPIRITUAL GIFTS

This chapter is designed to create an awareness and understanding of Spiritual gifts which will help you to navigate through life as a believer. The day you gave your life to God, you automatically had the ability to operate in Spiritual gifts. Spiritual gifts are not something to be afraid of but something to embrace. Spiritual gifts are not ancient but current and they are needed in the 21st century. Spiritual gifts are given by the Holy Spirit to point people to God, build the church and prepare believers for the coming of Jesus. This chapter will emphasize on the relevance of Spiritual gifts in the world we now live in. There are nine Spiritual gifts and other ministerial gifts mentioned in the bible that will be explored in this chapter. Even if you already know about Spiritual gifts, you might learn one or two things. His compassion is new every morning so is His revelation. I must admit that it was my first time to look deeper into the subject and the more I researched, the more the Holy Spirit revealed more to me. So, sit back, relax and enjoy this chapter.

What are Spiritual gifts and why are they important in the body of Christ? Spiritual gifts are given to individuals by the Holy Spirit to edify the body of Christ which is the church. They are not for us to keep to ourselves or use when we want but to glorify God. When you look at the physical body, all parts work together and if they do not work together there might be a problem. The hand cannot say to the body because I am better than the leg I am going to take a day off. The brain cannot decide to go on holiday and leave the rest of the body hanging. It is the responsibility of all parts of the body to make sure that the body remains in good condition. I remember the day I was diagnosed with Lupus (immune system fighting against itself), I was devastated knowing that the immune system that was meant to work for me and protect me will now be attacking me. Spiritual gifts are similar to our immune system. They keep the church of God together in unity and one spirit. Spiritual gifts are essential and they should work together for the body of Christ and not against each other. As much as spiritual gifts are given to individuals, they are also a collective gift to help believers get ready for the coming back of Jesus. There is no preference in the gift, each one is unique and there is no reason to be jealous of each other's gift (**Galatians6:4-6**). Think about our Lord Jesus, even though He had equal status with God, He always referenced and involved His father in everything He did.

I believe Spiritual gifts are already in our DNA, waiting to be activated when we decide to follow God. The bible says **"He knew us before He formed us (Romans 8:29).** A perfect example is my son AP. He was 6 months old when my midwife told me that the groaning sound he made was his personality and there was nothing medically wrong with him. However, as AP grew older the temperament and personality became more apparent. Who he is and will become was already inside of him when he was born. He is very confident when it comes to what he wants to do and it is difficult to persuade him to do otherwise. His confidence is unusual and can sometimes be mistaken as pride or arrogance. That gift of the confident spirit was already there even though he had not recognised or discovered it yet. In fact I believe our personality gives birth to Spiritual gifts. Looking back at my childhood personality and what I do now, they complement each other. When I was younger, I did not understand why I behaved the way I did but as I grew older I could see where my passion for some things came from. If you are wandering how you can receive Spiritual gifts, the Holy Spirit is the one that apportions these gifts and **Acts 19** explains how the Holy Spirit came on the disciples with the spiritual gifts when they received baptism in the name of Jesus: **There he found some disciples and asked them, "Did you receive the Holy Spirit when you believed?" They answered, "No, we have not even heard that there is a Holy Spirit." So Paul asked, "Then what baptism did you receive?" "John's baptism," they replied. Paul said, "John's baptism was a baptism of repentance. He told the people to believe in the one coming after him, that is, in Jesus." On hearing this, they were baptized in the name of the Lord Jesus. When Paul placed his hands on them, the Holy Spirit came on them, and they spoke in tongues and prophesied. There were about twelve men in all (Verse2-7).**

How do I know I have Spiritual gifts? The spirit will make it known to you through the word, dreams, vision and when others testify about it. In as much as you have the gift, it still needs to be activated, nurtured and enhanced as you use it. Sometimes, some people with spiritual insight i.e. spiritual mentors can tell you what your gift is. However, the fact that you are told that you have a gift is not enough, you need to recognise it yourself and make sure it is used for

Godly purposes. After you discover that you have a gift, ask the Holy Spirit to help you to understand how to use it. Some gifts are natural to some individuals who do not even see Spiritual gifts as separate to their personality. Remember, anyone can have a gift but not everyone will use it to glorify God. Use all that you have to honour the one who gave it to you as you do not know which of your personality God wants to use and when He wants to use it for His glory. **Just as you do not know the way and path of the wind or how the bones are formed in the womb of a pregnant woman, even so you do not know the activity of God who makes all things (Ecclesiastes11:5).**

I love gifts, especially free gifts/ special offers. I like the free offers sent to my phone but find them frustrating at times because of the long forms you have to fill in which is not sometimes a guarantee to receive the gift. Spiritual gifts on the other hand are yours as long as you want them and walk in God's ways. You do not have to fill a form or answer any questions, it comes directly to you and you do not need someone else to deliver it to you. There is no hidden agenda. There is a story in the bible that tells us that the gift of the Spirit is not for sale. A Spiritual gift is free, you do not have to pay for it or give something to get it. When Simon (the sorcerer) saw the miracles performed by Philip and the apostles, he gave his life to Christ and was baptised but greed got in the way of his understanding and he offered the Apostles money so that he could receive the same power as the apostle but was rebuked by Peter

(Acts8:18-24). I pray that your desire and motives for the spiritual gifts will be pure, holy and glorify God.

Now, let's explore each Spiritual gift, what it means and how it will bless individuals and the church.

To one person the Spirit gives the ability to give wise advice; to another the same Spirit gives a message of special knowledge. The same Spirit gives great faith to another, and to someone else the one Spirit gives the gift of healing. He gives one person the power to perform miracles, and another the ability to prophesy. He gives someone else the ability to discern whether a message is from the Spirit of God or from another spirit. Still another person is given the ability to speak in unknown languages, while another is given the ability to interpret what is being said. It is the one and only Spirit who distributes all these gifts. He alone decides which gift each person should have. (1Corinthians12:7-11 NLT).

WORD OF WISDOM: This is the ability to give wise advice. Solomon was a great example of wisdom in the Old Testament. Kings and Queens in his time came from far and near to acquire wisdom from him. Many brought gifts and even helped to build a house for God. Wise advice opened favours, opportunities and wealth to him **(1Kings5-10).** Our Lord Jesus is our greatest example of wisdom in the New Testament. At the age of 12, He was wise enough to give words of wisdom to those older than Him in the temple while some of the boys of His age would have had to seek their parents' permission do so. It is at 13 years when Jewish boys are considered to become accountable for their actions (when they become bar mitzvah). His parents searched for Him for three days before they finally found Him in the temple courts, sitting among the teachers, listening and asking questions. Everyone who heard Him was amazed at His understanding and He grew in wisdom, stature and in favour with God and men **(Luke2:41-52).** This gift should not be mistaken for intelligence/education/status. Nicodemus was a Jewish leader but still came to Jesus for more teaching **(John3).** The gift is not necessary given because you are at a certain age or a pastor or because you are the head of the family but because the Holy Spirit wants you to have the gift.

How would I know I have the gift? People around you will testify of how great your word of wisdom has blessed them. When Queen Sheba visited King Solomon and saw the King's wisdom, the house he built, the food on his table, the seating of his officials, his cupbearer and the robes of the servants who attended to her, she was overwhelmed. She told the King that the report she heard about his achievement were true and she saw how happy his officials and the people around him were. Above all she gave praise to the God of Solomon and blessed the King with gold, many spices and precious stones **(1King10:1-10).** The bible says: **your gift will make room for you and bring you before great men (Proverbs 18:16).** The gift of the word of wisdom also points the world to God as it did with Queen Sheba and made people to turn to their maker. The word of wisdom propels the church to the right direction and make the people who do not believe in God want to know more about Him.

The word of wisdom is not how eloquent you speak but how people are blessed by what you say. My son AS is what I refer to as a 'different breed' from me in regards to personality. He is calm and attentive to details especially from babies. From an early age I have had to surrender him to God. He is not irrational and doesn't do things in haste like me. He takes his time to make decisions and the decisions he has made in the past have proven to be good. He is full of wisdom and his judgement of character has helped me to become a better person. I remember asking him something and he responded with calmness saying 'can he get back to me on a subject'. I was like who taught him that and I was fuming. I thought; 'why can't he just tell me now?'. At the age of 4, he told an adult (in a calm manner) that he should apologise to me because he hurt me. How did he know how to say things like that? At the age of 14, he told someone who was older than him in a conversation that he should 'breathe in insult and breathe out the praise'. How did he come up with a sentence like that? His personality always attracts young and older people to him. I often ask his opinion about things and he gives his understanding where he can. In my observation, people with this gift are calm and humble. They do not have to shout to be heard. Words that come out of their mouth are like magnet that attracts people to them. People search for them rather than they search for people just like the story about Solomon and Our Lord Jesus. The gift blesses the church and everyone around them. In conclusion, the body of Christ needs this gift in order for the people to flourish in their spheres of life and help the church not to make the same mistakes our fore fathers made in the bible. **See the book of Proverbs for more reading on wisdom.**

SPECIAL KNOWLEDGE: The word of knowledge is the word God puts in the mouth of the giver to speak through the Holy Spirit. It might be a scripture, a vision, a song, dream or words. In the atmosphere of worship, anointing and power, God will talk to His people. The words given can be directly or indirectly to people's circumstances. So therefore, it is important for the church to pay attention when the word of knowledge is given because it might be a warning/correction/direction for the season or the future. You can write or record the word as it is being given so that you can listen to it later but I find the writing a distraction as some important words can be missed. The giver does not necessarily need to know the receiver before he/she gives word of knowledge. I want you to know that both the giver and the receiver are in the same boat as none of them know what the Holy Spirit will say. The giver is as vulnerable to give the words as well as the receiver. The giver is directed by the Holy Spirit to deliver the words God wants to reveal to His children. So, if you are the giver just relax and let the Holy Spirit work in and through you to perfect His work. I have received and given a word of knowledge in the past, that I did not understand or was not related to me at that moment but as I inquired further from the Lord the Holy Spirit gave me insight and understanding into the words spoken.

The word of knowledge is not a memory verse or a word you have planned in your head to say but the word is spoken in power and authority even the person has no choice but to say it out. One day in a meeting, the Holy Spirit gave a word of knowledge but as I got to a particular part, I felt hesitant about what the Holy Spirit wanted me to say because I was not sure if what I was saying was right. Then, I began to say out aloud "why are you resisting what I want you to say, be not afraid, I am with you". I finally obeyed and I am glad I did because unknown to me it was the word the person needed at that moment. When the Lord gives you a word, do not hold back just deliver the message. You are a messenger and the word of knowledge you give is spontaneous and relevant to the person you give it to. At Pentecost, Peter stood up and began to speak about Jesus boldly. Prior to this everyone was afraid to talk about Jesus or talk about His resurrection for the fear of the Pharisees and Jewish leaders. So when Peter stood up with courage and boldness to address the people that day, he was speaking by the auction of the Holy Spirit. Remember, they had not experienced the Holy Spirit before, Jesus only told them to go to Jerusalem **(Acts2).** It seems that people with this gift speak with boldness and courage when they open their mouth to speak the word God has given them.

From my understanding, I believe that people with the word of knowledge have the ability to say what is in the heart of God in order to bless the church, warn about disasters to come and to reveal who God is to His church. We see this when Jesus revealed the life of a Samaritan woman at Jacob's well. Even though

He was tired He did not resist the urge to speak to a strange woman. The word of knowledge spoken by our Lord Jesus brought salvation and deliverance to the woman and the entire town. Jesus did not know the woman and moreover she was a Samaritan. During that time, the Jews felt superior when comparing themselves with the Samaritans so the disciples were surprised when they came back from fetching lunch that Jesus was talking to her in the first place **(John 4).** The revelation was not only for the woman and the town but it was recorded and now we and many generations can read about it as well. People with this gift have a close relationship with God hence they are able to know the mystery and hidden secrets that no one knows. The church needs people with this gift especially in the world where people have turned away from the God that created them. A miracle like the Samaritan woman's story will bring people to God and add more people to the church which is what happened at Pentecost and during the time of the disciples of Jesus.

GREAT FAITH/FAITHFULNESS: Now faith is the substance of things hoped for, the evidence of things not seen (Hebrews11:1). Faith is the key to answered prayers, the bible says without faith it is impossible to please God **(Hebrews11:6).**I believe that everyone who believes in God has some level of faith to be able to walk the journey of faith. It takes faith to believe you are healed when you are still sick. The bible says, even if you have small faith like the mustard seed your prayer will be answered

(**Luke17:6**). It takes the gift of faithfulness to follow Christ, believe the God you have not seen and be totally devoted to him for the rest of your life. However, this great faith that I am talking about is another level of faith where you believe something uncommon or extra ordinary will happen. It seems people with this gift see or believe the impossible. They have the faith to believe and act based on what they see in the spirit whether it makes sense naturally or not. There are many examples of people with the gift of faith in the bible but I will mention a few.

It took faith for **Moses** to reassure and convince the people of Israel that God wanted them to be free from the Egyptians. The Israelites had just been delivered from the oppressor by a man who told them that God wanted them to leave Egypt. They were faced with a red sea before them, the Egyptian army behind them and they were terrified. Moses on the other hand was not informed or given an escape plan in case anything unusual occurred on the way. He was an ordinary man like you and I doing what God told him to do. It took faith for Moses to see beyond the chaos and believe that God was going to fight for the Israelites and will deliver them even though Moses had not received further instructions about how to deal with the situation when he told them (**Exodus14:10-22**). My question is how did he know that God would deliver them that day? I suppose it was due to the plagues he performed before they left Egypt. But the Israelites saw the plagues too, how come they did not believe like Moses? Even Aaron and Miriam doubted Moses at one point. What makes Moses different? He knew God and trusted that He was going to do what He said

He would do and He does not change. Moses could see beyond the red sea and could see what others could not see. He believed the uncommon, unusual and extraordinary God who knows the end before the beginning.

Abraham is another great man of faith. He listened to the God he had not seen and left his family to embark on a journey to a promise land he did not have full details about. Abraham was 75years when he started his journey of becoming a great man and powerful father of a nation. At ninety nine years old, the Lord appeared to Abraham and told him if he walked faithfully and blameless before Him, He will give him the land he had shown him. Abraham finally had the son he was promised at a very old age and was told to sacrifice the child to God. Eventually, he saw the land but he did not live there **(Genesis12-15).**

By faith, **Noah** built an ark because God told him He was going to wipe out the human race and there was going to be a flood. It was rare for God to speak or confide in humanity at that time because of their wickedness. But Noah found favour with the Lord and He revealed His plans to him. Noah had probably not seen that kind of rain in his entire life or seen an ark let alone know how to build one before and to cap it all, Noah had to tell the people that floods were coming. I cannot imagine the humiliation but he did it **(Genesis6-9)** because he believed God even though it did not make sense to him.

It appears to me that people with this gift listen and follow instructions. They are willing to do anything for God. They do not mind to travel across the world to carry out God's mission. They are not perfect as we see in the life of Abraham, Moses and Noah. They are ordinary men like you and I. In my observation, people with this gift are content and there is this calmness about them. I suppose they have to be if they have to rely totally on God for guidance and direction. Timing is not an issue as long as the Lord is with them. My sister (Bunmi) has this gift and I always admire her courage and boldness. She has been to places like Tibet and Nepal for missionary work even though she knew that if she was captured she will be jailed or killed. By observing her I also noticed that people with this gift are not afraid to do anything for God even though it is beyond what they are comfortable with. During the Covid19 pandemic, she deliberately asked to work on a ward with Covid19 patients in order to help those who were really sick. An extraordinary faith that requires patience, tolerance, endurance and calmness. I had a dream once which I only told her recently (2020). In the dream I was rescuing people from the building wreckage; all of a sudden I heard that my sister was in the accident that caused the building to collapse. I left everything I was doing to go and look for my sister. People were telling me that she might be among the dead but I ignored them. Like a ferocious lion I bagged into rooms where victims were kept. When I finally saw my sister, she had no legs but she was hopping about smiling and helping people around her. She did not recognise me at first until I mentioned our mother's name. I was sad for her but she was giving hope to others, reassuring them it will be okay. **Read more about people of faith in Hebrews11**

HEALING: The gift speaks for itself. Every believer is given power and authority to heal the sick, the broken hearted and set captives free **(Isaiah61:1-4)**. However, there are some believers who demonstrate the gift of healing. Recently, I watched Kenneth and Gloria Copeland messages to lift up my faith and I believe they both have the gift of healing. I had been praying for weeks about my recovery but when I started listening to their messages and prayer of confession, my faith was lifted and I was able to receive the healing Yahweh has already given to me. I am still amazed by the story of Lazarus in the bible, the corpse of 4 days old brought back to life. Of course I know He is the Lord and He can do all things but I also know that when He was on earth He was fully man which means He had to trust His father that Lazarus will come back to life. However, research shows that between 30-180 seconds of oxygen deprivation you can lose consciousness, at one-minute brain cells will begin to die, at three minutes, neurons will suffer more extensive damage, and brain damage becomes more likely. At five minutes, death becomes imminent, at 10 minutes, even if the brain remains alive, a coma and lasting brain damage are almost inevitable and at 15 minutes, survival becomes nearly impossible. Yet, Jesus waited for 4 days before He went Lazarus's grave. I cannot imagine the state of the corpse or the cells and neurons. When Jesus called Lazarus from the dead and he back to life. There is nothing impossible for our Lord.

I believe people with this gift have the ability to pray for the sick and they instantly recover. Signs and wonders usually follow them. We saw this with Peter, Philip and the Apostle in the book of **Acts.** Healing is given by the Holy Spirit; you cannot buy or sell it. To the people with the gift and those that receive it is a mystery, no wonder Simon wanted to buy it in **Acts 8**. Do not be deceived by those who demand that you buy oil, a drink or a handkerchief before you can be healed. By his stripes you are already healed through the body and the blood of Jesus. His healing is free and given by the Holy Spirit. Also, do not allow the gift to get into your head thinking you heal by your power. The gift is given and can be taken from you if it does not glorify God. In the bible we see how glory and anointing departed from kings because they forgot the one who put them in the position. Do not take credit for what you did not do. The Lord will not share His glory with anyone. There are instances whereby healing does not manifest. It is not necessarily something you have done or you have not done or the sin of the past. The Lord loves you and He has forgiven you. **He does not treat us as our sins deserve or repay us according to our iniquities (Psalms 103:10**). However, if you have committed a sin, repent and ask the Father to forgive you. The following are some of the things that can hinder healing: doubt, lack of faith, complaining, you do not want to be healed because you have accepted that your condition is fate. There are also instances in the bible whereby Jesus ignored the people's unbelief and healed them anyway. For those who desire the gift, it is not limited by age or status, if you desire it and the Holy Spirit wants you to have it, it is yours. There are so many schools of healing around the world, I am sure one will be closer to you and give it a go. It is also important to be where your gift will be effective. For instance, if you have or desire this gift but the fellowship/meetings you attend do not believe or recognise or teach on it, how can you bless anyone? How precious will it be if the gift of healing is recognised and understood in every meeting or Sunday service? Signs and wonders will be seen as in the times of the Apostles and the world we know that there is God. The church is a hospital for everyone that comes to receive healing to get well. **"You are the light of the world. A town built on a hill cannot be hidden. Neither do people light a lamp and put it under a bowl. Instead they put it on its stand, and it gives light to everyone in the house. In the same way, let your light shine before others, that they may see your good deeds and glorify your Father in heaven. (Matthew 5:14-16).**

PERFORM MIRACLES/MIRACULOUS POWER: This gift is similar to the gift of healing. The spiritual gift to perform miracles is a divine will of God and it is given by the Holy Spirit to certain people in church. Jesus performed many miracles when he was on earth, more than those recorded in scripture **(John 20:30-31.** Jesus is not the only one who performed miracles, the Apostles regularly performed miracles of all kinds including casting out demons, healing, raising people from the dead and much more **(Acts 2, 3, 5, 9, 13, 19).** Miraculous power is given by God to the church in order to reveal His presence and glory, as well as increase our faith and boldness. Also, the gift creates a sense of awe, wonder and reverence of God which brings more people to the kingdom of God. In my opinion, people with the spiritual gift of performing miracles have a measure of faith to believe what the Lord is telling them to do or say. They believe that God is Sovereign and understand that He will show His power when and how He wants. They listen to the prompting of the Holy Spirit and allow the Holy Spirit to work in and through them. Jesus used a variety of methods to perform miracles during His time**: He laid hands (Matthew9:18-19, 23-26), Spat on the ground and made mud (John 9:1-6), Fed 5000 people (Mark6:35-44) Turned water to wine (John 2:1-11**). This gift is accompanied by prayer and sometimes fasting in order for God to reveal His glory to His people. In the atmosphere of praise and worship, miracles are performed, His miraculous power is seen by those who do not know Him and the Holy Spirit will move among the people. **After they prayed, the place where they were meeting was shaken. And they were all filled with the Holy Spirit and spoke the word of God boldly. (Acts4:31)**

People with this gift I believe, do not necessarily need to touch or speak to people before miracles happen, their presence is enough to heal the sick. The woman with the issue of blood just needed to touch the hem of Jesus's garment and she was healed **(Mark5:24-34)** Peter's shadow healed the sick: **Nevertheless, more and more men and women believed in the Lord and were added to their number. As a result, people brought the sick into the streets and laid them on beds and mats so that at least Peter's** shadow might fall on some of them as he passed by. Crowds gathered also from the towns around Jerusalem, bringing their sick and those tormented by impure spirits, and all of them were healed. (Acts5:14-16). This gift will attract different kinds of people and it is important to pay attention to God's principles. People with the gift must not open the door to fame/greed/pride/ arrogance/anything that will make them think that the miracles performed are by their power and they should avoid seeking for more powers but seek more of God's presence. Their heart must be pure and holy without blemish and stain and they must remember the gift of miracles is to glorify God **(Acts 1:8, Galatians 3:5).**

PROPHESY: The gift of prophecy was in fact rated second out of the gifts God placed on the church by Paul and should not be treated with contempt **(1 Thessalonians 5:20).** In Paul's writing he puts a lot of emphasis on prophecy: **Follow the way of love and eagerly desire gifts of the Spirit, especially prophecy. For anyone who speaks in tongues does not speak to people but to God. Indeed, no one understands them; they utter mysteries by the spirit. But the one who prophesies speaks to people for their strengthening, encouraging and comfort. But the one who prophesies edifies the church. I would like every one of you to speak in tongues, but I would rather have you prophesy. The one who prophesies is greater than the one who speaks in tongues, unless someone interprets, so that the church may be edified.**

(1Corinthians14:1-5) The Holy Spirit gives the gift of prophecy to some believers to reveal the heart of God and to edify the church. This gift benefits both believers and unbelievers and is a sign that God is truly among His church **(1 Corinthians 14:22-25)**. I believe that people with this gift listen to the prompting of the Holy Spirit and the needs of the church. I have observed that people with this gift are humble and continually study the scriptures in order to test the revelations before speaking. When they do speak, they allow others to weigh what is said through them against the scriptures, pray about it and interpret the message accordingly. In this way the church continues to grow together in unity **(1 Corinthians 14:4, 26)**. People with this gift are not afraid to tell the truth. Jehoshaphat told King Ahab to consult a prophet when they wanted to go to war. All the prophets in the land consulted (400) told him to go to war but Jehoshaphat insisted they try other prophets. Reluctantly, King Ahab invited Micaiah and Micaiah was not afraid to tell the king what the Lord told him will happen to him if he goes to war **(2Chronicles18)**.

There are great prophets in the bible such as **Elijah (1King 18-19), Elisha (2Kings7-8), Samuel, Jeremiah, Isaiah, Amos, Ezekiel, Nehemiah, Hosea, Malachi, Zechariah, Haggai, Habakkuk, Micah etc.** These books of the bible are worth reading for more understanding about the prophets. The bible also warns us several times to be aware and stay away from false prophets and test what is said against the scripture **(1 Thessalonians 5)**. False prophets are people who say things the Holy Spirit did not send them to. They lie and deceive people for their own gain. There is a punishment for those who distract God's children and cause them to turn away from Him. Do not be used by the devil to give a false message. Be sure you are sent by the Holy Spirit. Do not speak what you do not recognise. You can only recognise the word of God by getting to know Him. Jesus recognised the voice of the devil when He was tempted by him and was determined not to compromise. Adam and Eve on the other hand did not recognise the devil when he came to tempt them in the Garden of Eden or should I say they under estimated how crafty the devil is and became separated from God. Know the voice of your Father, refrain from following the voice of the stranger. There is nothing that gives me more pleasure than to show you scriptures about false prophets: **This is what the Lord Almighty says: Do not listen to what the prophets are prophesying to you; they fill you with false hopes. They speak visions from their own minds, not from the mouth of the LORD. (Jeremiah23:16).**

Dear friends, do not believe every spirit, but test the spirits to see whether they are from God, because many false prophets have gone out into the world. This is how you can recognize the Spirit of God: Every spirit that acknowledges that Jesus Christ has come in the flesh is from God, but every spirit that does not acknowledge Jesus is not from God. This is the spirit of the antichrist, which you have heard is coming and even now is already in the world. You, dear children, are from God and have overcome them, because the one who is in you is greater than the one who is in the

world. They are from the world and therefore speak from the viewpoint of the world, and the world listens to them. We are from God, and whoever knows God listens to us; but whoever is not from God does not listen to us. This is how we recognize the Spirit of truth and the spirit of falsehood. (1John4:1-6). Also, Matthew7:15-20 says: "Watch out for false prophets. They come to you in sheep's clothing, but inwardly they are ferocious wolves. By their fruit you will recognize them. Do people pick grapes from thornbushes, or figs from thistles? Likewise, every good tree bears good fruit, but a bad tree bears bad fruit. A good tree cannot bear bad fruit, and a bad tree cannot bear good fruit. Every tree that does not bear good fruit is cut down and thrown into the fire. Thus, by their fruit you will recognize them.

DISCERNMENT: The spiritual gift of discernment is a gift given to believers to recognise or distinguish between spirits **(1 Corinthians 12:10).** Those with this gift have the ability to discern good and evil as God sees it not human definition of it. As we spend time with God and our relationship deepens, we begin to know what we are called to do in the world. The bible says we are of the world but not of it. As a matter of fact, I believe all believers should be able to discern good and evil especially in the world where lies are justified over the truth. Again, like the rest of the spiritual gifts, this gift requires constantly spending time in God's presence and to know your Father well enough in order to recognise when you are confronted with lies. **In fact, though by this time you ought to be teachers, you need someone to teach you the**

elementary truths of God's word all over again. You need milk, not solid food! Anyone who lives on milk, being still an infant, is not acquainted with the teaching about righteousness. But solid food is for the mature, who by constant use have trained themselves to distinguish good from evil (Hebrews 5:12-14). Our Lord Jesus is the great example of discernment. He recognised the heart of people when they wanted to get Him into trouble with the law. He knew his enemies and He was careful around them. Jesus was not afraid of His enemies but He applied lots of wisdom to answer their questions. Most of the time, He spoke in parables to the people but spent time explaining the parables to His disciples. When He perceived that the people tried to put words in His mouth or were twisting His words like the journalists do, He remained focussed at all times and used the word of God to answer the questions in their heart and made them to judge for themselves if the situation was right or wrong. These are few scriptures where Jesus perceived what was going on in the heart of men **(Matthew9:4, 12:25, 22:18 Luke5:22, 6:8, 11:17, Acts15:8).**

We also saw how Jesus healed or prayed for people even though the people did not ask or expect it because He perceived in His heart that it was needed i.e. the man who was lame for 38 years **(John 5)**. I used to tell everyone everything about my life until during one of our devotions my children told me I had no filter. As I spent time with Yahweh, the Holy Spirit began to teach me how to be discreet, discern who I hang out with and information that I share with people. The more you know Him the more you begin to sense what is not good or evil around you. **But they will never follow a stranger; in fact, they will run away from him because they do not recognize a stranger's voice. My sheep listen to my voice; I know them, and they follow me. (John10:5, 27)**Do not be fooled that some believers will not try to harm you. I believed this for many years until I was hurt by those closer to me. In one of our family devotions one of my sons said "he does not allow what people say get to him". I wish someone had told me this long time ago, I would not have exposed myself to danger but thanks be to Yahweh for His grace. Those who wear glasses need them to see, those who wear hearing aids need them to hear, those with sight impairment use their senses to perceive things around them. It is said that majority of humans do not make use of all their senses but concentrate on the ones they are used to. Let your do what it is created to do. I have noticed that people who are left handed tend to use both of their hands than those who use their right hands. In 2012, I could not use my right hand to do most things so I had to learn to depend on my left hand. In the beginning, it was hard because I was not used to it but I began to appreciate what my right hand does for me. Even though I intended to use my left hand more, I forgot about it immediately I regained strength in my right hand.

Believers are not robots or mind readers! I believe this gift will equip, protect and prevent us from danger. With discerning spirits we will be able to see, hear and perceive what is going on around us and to know the heart of God when we make choices and decisions. Believers need this gift to guard themselves from people whose intention is to harm them. Many times the bible warns us to be careful, guide our heart and test all spirits. Do not deliberately walk into danger just because you cannot discern what is going on around you. The Holy Spirit will help us to perceive every spirit that is not from God and we will listen and obey His voice. How do I recognise a discerning spirit? It can be a strange feeling about a place or that strong feeling when you refuse to sign a business deal for no reason. People of the world call it instinct or to follow your heart. I believe most believers operate in this gift but there are some people that are given this gift specifically to fulfil the purposes of God. The gift of discernment also enables certain Christians to clearly recognize and distinguish between God, Satan, the world, and the flesh in a given situation. The church needs those with this gift to warn believers in times of danger or keep them from being led astray by false teaching. The more we remain and abide in Him, the more we will continue to hear Him and make right decisions. In my opinion, people with this gift will be quick to listen and slow to speak, making it possible for them to wait patiently and weigh information before making decisions. They do not make rash or irrational decisions. However, there are times when the person with this gift will make irrational decisions to protect people from harm and they might not understand why they are behaving a certain way towards something. For instance: **A Pastor from Lebanon yielded to the voice of the Holy Spirit on the 4th of August 2020 and saved 34 staff and 240 children of his church from a massive explosion in Beirut. He told CBN News that while they were praying that Tuesday morning, he felt anxious, unease, sadness and** anger but he did not know why. He was rude to the people and told them to go home and come back on Sunday. His members thought he has lost his mind because they were in the middle of a meeting, and later they needed to provide food for thousands but instead he insisted that everyone should pack everything up and go home. His obedience and discerning spirit saved his member from an explosion that killed more than 200 people, thousand injured and many became homeless that afternoon.

SPEAKING IN TONGUES: This is the ability to speak in unknown words/language which is sometimes referred to as 'Heavenly language'. This is an utterance of prayer or words to glorify God. It is a language that is unknown to the speaker but known only to the one you are speaking to. **For anyone who speaks in tongues does not speak to people but to God. Indeed, no one understands them; they utter mysteries by the Spirit (1Corinthians14:2).**To understand this gift properly, we need to explore the history of language in the human race. In the Garden of Eden, mankind had one language which was how they communicated and communed with God. Unfortunately, this relationship changed when Adam and Eve sinned against God and was banished from the Garden of Eden. Mankind continued to have one language **(see Genesis 11)** until when they conspired to build a tower in Babel because they wanted to make a name for themselves and replace God in their hearts. God altered their language and the people were dispersed throughout the earth. Then God chose people with one language to bring Him glory and draw mankind back to Himself. Through Abraham the nation of Israel was established, the hebrew language was used to communicate God's word to the nations. However, the rest of the world did not speak or understand this language then but on the day of Pentecost, the pouring out of the Holy Spirit reversed the curse that divided the languages and brought the languages together **(Acts 2)**. I believe when we finally get to heaven, every nation, tribe and tongue will join together to praise God with one language again. **After this, I looked and there before me was a great multitude that no one could count, from every nation, tribe, people and language, standing before the throne and before the Lamb. They were wearing white robes and were holding palm branches in their hands. And they cried out in a loud voice: "Salvation belongs to our God, who sits on the throne, and to the Lamb." (Revelation 7:9-10)**. I believe when completeness comes, we will all go back to speaking one language that everyone will understand **(corinthians13:8-10).** At the moment the gift of speaking in tongues is only partial to believers who can speak it and an interpreter is needed for it to be understood and to edify the church.

Now, brothers and sisters, if I come to you and speak in tongues, what good will I be to you, unless I bring you some revelation or knowledge or prophecy or word of instruction? Even in the case of lifeless things that make sounds, such as the pipe or harp, how will anyone know what tune is being played unless there is a distinction in the

notes? Again, if the trumpet does not sound a clear call, who will get ready for battle? So it is with you. Unless you speak intelligible words with your tongue, how will anyone know what you are saying? You will just be speaking into the air. Undoubtedly there are all sorts of languages in the world, yet none of them is without meaning. If then I do not grasp the meaning of what someone is saying, I am a foreigner to the speaker, and the speaker is a foreigner to me. So it is with you. Since you are eager for gifts of the Spirit, try to excel in those that build up the church. For this reason the one who speaks in a tongue should pray that they may interpret what they say. For if I pray in a tongue, my spirit prays, but my mind is unfruitful. So what shall I do? I will pray with my spirit, but I will also pray with my understanding; I will sing with my spirit, but I will also sing with my understanding. Otherwise when you are praising God in the Spirit, how can someone else, who is now put in the position of an inquirer, say "Amen" to your thanksgiving, since they do not know what you are saying? You are giving thanks well enough, but no one else is edified. (1Conrinthians14:6-17)

I believe what Paul was saying in this text is that, when tongues are spoken in a meeting or church gatherings, there needs to be an interpreter for the visiting unbeliever and those people who do not speak in tongues to feel included in the meeting. This is the reason why I believe we all need to activate our spiritual gifts so that they can be useful for our church services, fellowship, connect groups and meetings. A man was invited to a party and was told it would be fun and lots of people would be there. When he got to the party he realised he was the only one who did not speak the language everyone was speaking. He could not understand or communicate; he felt embarrassed and left out. So, it is important to put this in mind when organising a Holy Ghost party. Speaking in tongues has its advantage and disadvantage. The advantage of the gift is that it edifies you, you can use it when you do not know what to say in prayer, only God understands what you are saying and even the enemy does not understand it either. It's like your secret code to your Father. Majority of times when my children talk to each other I do not have a clue as to what they are saying even though they are speaking in English. The disadvantage of the gift is that you do not know what you are saying unless you have the gift of interpretation of tongues. Tongues can be human languages such as those heard in **(Acts 2)** or languages no one understands **(1 Corinthians 14:2).**Tongues are not "ecstatic speeches" but orderly and controlled by the one speaking **(1 Corinthians 14:27-28, 33, 39-40).**Tongues should not be forbidden in church or Christian meetings **(1 Corinthians 14:39).** In **Acts 2** people spoke in the language that they have never spoken before and those around them could understand what they were saying. I used to say that I cannot live in a country where people do not speak English because I am unable to hear or speak another language but recently I have the desire to speak in other languages especially in meetings where not everyone can speak English. How awesome would it be if God stopped a meeting to speak to His children in their local language by using someone who has never spoken the language before to minister to them? That would be a personal encounter that will be cherished for life. It is also possible that those who speak in many languages have the gift because every gift comes from the Father. I believe that not every believer will receive this gift and it is not a requirement or a sign of salvation. The gift of tongues is to glorify God and edify the church which is you and I. Therefore, it is important to use the gift properly with pure motives and by the prompting of the Holy Spirit. **(See aslo1 Corinthians 12:10, 30, 14:4, Acts 2:4, Acts 19:6).**

INTERPRETATION OF TONGUES: The gift of interpretation is a supernatural ability to understand and explain messages uttered in an unknown language **(1 Corinthians 12:10).** The Greek word for interpretation is **"Hermeneia"** and it simply means to interpret, explain, or expound messages that cannot be understood in a natural way. People with this gift should be present in our meetings so that when the Lord speaks through tongues, there is someone available to interpret. A man who desire/ has the gift of interpreting tongues should fellowship in a place where speaking in tongues is recognised in order to benefit the church. The gift is not a separate gift but an accompanying gift which means it cannot function on its own, without tongues **(1 Corinthians14:1-28).**Also, this gift is a revelatory gift, which means that God is the only one who can reveal the meaning of the words or messages spoken through the Holy Spirit and He will allow the interpreter to communicate its meaning to those who need to hear it. Like most of the spiritual gifts, interpretation has the effect of encouraging the church to love and serve God more deeply and effectively. A dream without interpretation is frustrating and can create anxiety, fear and rushed/bad decisions and choices. King Nebuchadnezzar was prosperous and great in his days. One day he had a dream that made him afraid and terrified. So He commanded all the magicians, enchanters, astrologers and diviners to come and interpret the dream but no one could interpret the dream except Daniel **(Daniel4:4-8).**

It is important to know that it is not necessarily that the person who speaks in tongues should interpret. One person can speak, another can interpret or both can be done by the same person as the Holy Spirit permits. People with this gift must be close to God and must be able to distinguish His voice in order to deliver what the spirit is saying accurately. You cannot assume this is what you think the spirit is saying, it must be accurate. I believe people with this gift are humble. For example, Joseph demonstrated this when Pharaoh had a dream that no one could interpret and Pharaoh told Joseph that he had heard that he could interpret his dreams but Joseph told him: **"I cannot do it," Joseph replied to Pharaoh, "but God will give Pharaoh the answer he desires." (Genesis41:16)**

It has been a great journey looking at these spiritual gifts. I have been tremendously blessed and have learnt so much. Journal your thoughts and research on anything that has confused you. I believe your pastor/leaders/mentors will be happy to help you with anything you do not understand. Now that we have looked at the Spiritual gifts mentioned in **1Corinthians12:8-10,** let's look at other gifts that were mentioned in **Romans12:6-8** and **Corinthians12:27-31** which are sometimes referred to as ministerial gifts. They are the gifts of Administration, Apostleship, Evangelism, Exhortation, Giving, Mercy, Pastor, Service and Teaching. Remember that every gift is given to us by the Holy Spirit to bless the body of Christ. It is our responsibility to look after these gifts and make sure they are used for what God intended them for. The bible says our gift will make room for us and bring us before great men. Do not allow the gift to make you arrogant that you forget the person who gave you the gift in the first place. Remain humble and allow your gift to be used as part of a team that honours the Father, Son and the Holy Spirit. As the trinity is one we also are to be one with the one who created us. **Paul encouraged us to: Be completely humble and gentle; be patient, bearing with one another in love. Make every effort to keep the unity of the Spirit through the bond of peace. There is one body and one Spirit, just as you were called to one hope when you were called; one Lord, one faith, one baptism; one God and Father of all, who is over all and through all and in all. But to each one of us grace has been given as Christ apportioned it (Ephesians4:2-7).**

ADMINISTRATION: The gift of administration in Greek is called **"kubernesis"** meaning **to steer or rule or govern.** The gift of Administration is part of the gifts needed in the body of Christ.

(1Corinthians12:27-28). The Holy Spirit gives this gift to guide and direct people towards a goal or destination. One of the disciples of Jesus that came to my mind and I believe has this gift is Peter. Jesus told Peter he was a rock and upon him He was going to build His church **(Matthew 16:18**) and He gave him the instruction to take care and feed His sheep **(John 21:16-17).** It was no surprise on the day of Pentecost when Peter stood up to address the people and point them to the right direction **(Acts 1&2).** Peter is the disciple who left his boat and followed Jesus **(Matthew4:18-20).** When no one knew who Jesus was it was Peter who spoke boldly that Jesus was the messiah **(Matthew16:13-17).** Peter is the one Jesus called Satan and told him to get behind Him. We also saw Peter's bravery when Jesus told him to come to Him and he walked on water **(Matthew14:22-29).** Peter was eager to do things, and was the first to speak up and not afraid to say what was on his mind. He is the one who denied Jesus three times **(John18:15-27)** and decided to go back fishing after Jesus's death, taking along the rest of the disciples **(John21:3).** When Jesus died there was no one to direct the people, all the disciples were scattered and the people were afraid to talk about Jesus due to fear of what the Jewish leaders would do to them. It was Peter who stood up and spoke to the people with boldness and courage **(Acts1&2).** It seems to me that people with this gift have some sort of organisational skills and are able to make sure things are in order. They can organize, direct, and implement plans to lead others in the various ministries of the Church. This gift is closely related to the gift of leadership, but is more of goal or task oriented.

APOSTLESHIP: Apostleship is an office of Apostle. Paul put Apostleship above the rest of the gift to emphasise the importance of an Apostle in the church **(1 Corinthians12:28).** Apostle means **"the sent one".** The apostles are the early followers of Jesus who carried Christian messages to the world i.e. the disciples. The Apostles were commissioned by Jesus to go into the world and equip them for the work of the ministry. **So Christ himself gave the apostles, the prophets, the evangelists, the pastors and teachers, to equip his people for works of service, so that the body of Christ may be built up until we are all unified in faith and in the knowledge of the Son of God and become mature, attaining to the whole measure of the fullness of Christ. (Ephesians4:11-12).** In the present day, I believe the mission of apostleship is to plant new ministries and churches, go into places where the Gospel is not preached. Apostles travel across different cultures to establish churches even in challenging environments where the Gospel is not allowed to be preached or where there is war or poverty. Wherever they go they develop leaders/ pastors and motivate others around them. They may also have other gifts which allow them to fulfil the work in the ministry. They are typical entrepreneurial and are able to take risks and perform difficult tasks which we saw with the apostles in the bible. People with this gift can be missionaries, church planters, Christian scholars, institutional leaders, and those leading multiple ministries of churches. Paul is a great example of apostleship. He planted churches in Corinth, Rome and Philipi.

EVANGELISM: This is the ability to clearly and effectively communicate the Gospel of Jesus Christ to others. The Greek word for evangelists is **"Euaggelistes"** which means **"one who brings good news."** The spiritual gift of evangelism was given to build up the body of Christ and to bring more souls to the kingdom **(Ephesians 4:11-12).** The word **"Evangelists"** can be found in **Acts 21:8 and 2 Timothy 4:5**. I believe people with this gift often have the burden for lost souls in their hearts and they will go out of their way to share the truth of the Gospel with them. In my observations, Evangelists are able to overcome the fear of rejection and they allow the Holy Spirit to lead them to engage with non-believers in meaningful conversations about Jesus. People with this gift are able to communicate with all types of people and relate well with those who do not know God **(Act 9, 10)**. If it was in our time Paul, Philip, Barnabas, Peter, Stephen, John, and many more in the bible will be considered Evangelists. I will advise that you research more about the gift if you are burdened for lost souls and you want them to come to know Christ (See recommended books).

Let's digress a bit to our calling as believers

All Christians are called to evangelize and reach out to the lost to share the Gospel of Jesus Christ **(Matthew 28:18-20).** As believers we should have the burden for lost souls in our hearts and the desire to see people come to know Jesus. **Romans 10:14** says: **But how can they call on him to save them unless they believe in him? And how can they believe in him if they have never heard about him? And how can**

they hear about him unless someone tells them?
As much as I believe that people will come to know Christ based on what they see in me, I also believe that the things of this world have blinded people to see God clearly i.e. money, fame, good medical facilities, inheritance, wealth, prosperity, good jobs, career. Some believe the gospel of Christ is for the poor, sick, disadvantage people but it is for everyone. For God so loved the world that he gave his only son to die for the world **(John3:3)** and unless a man be born again they cannot come to the kingdom **(John3:16)**. Even though some believe there is God, they are too busy to commit to Him. I am aware that not everyone will come to know Christ but as believers we should be able to say like Paul that his life was not worth more than to complete the tasks that the Lord had given him which was to testify of the good news of Christ **(Acts20:24).** I believe our stories and lives have changed many lives and we are still changing lives but we need to seriously look around us and be concerned about souls crossing to hell daily. Our loved ones are missing out because we are waiting for them to make the first move. The belief that being good, kind, loving and compassionate is the only way to bring people to the Lord is not enough, there are some people in the world who believe in the same principles and they are not believers. I believe the walk of faith is not only by our good works but God's grace.

For it is by grace you have been saved, through faith and this is not from yourselves, it is the gift of God, not by works, so that no one can boast. For we are God's handiwork, created in Christ

Jesus to do good works, which God prepared in advance for us to do (Ephesians2:8-9). It is time to wake up and embrace what we are called to do. Most of our friends know we are believers but how many have given their life to God because of that? Many may not walk through the door of a church but our compassion and fervency to reach out to them with the gospel of truth will save them where they are. Do not get me wrong there are friends, colleagues, neighbours and family that I am still praying for to give their life to Christ but I know that one day I will receive a call about their encounter with Jesus but until then I believe I need to do more in reaching out to souls. The Holy Spirit will give us insight if we are willing and if we open our hearts to understanding. The Lord promised that, **"wisdom" will enter our hearts, "knowledge" will be pleasant to our soul, "discretion" will protect us and "understanding" will guard us (Proverbs2:10-11**). The book of **Acts** is the best place to begin if you desire to take your evangelism further. I pray that the Lord will give you the passion to really go out of your way to tell everyone you meet about the gospel of Jesus Christ.

EXHORTATION: The gift of exhortation/encouragement. The Greek word for this gift is "Parakaleo" which in the original manuscripts is translated as counsel, comfort, console, exhort, call upon, encourage and to strengthen. Paul in his writing commanded Titus and Timothy to use this gift **(Titus1:9, 2, 2 Timothy 4:2)**. I believe people with this gift have the ability to come alongside another person as they grow in their faith to strengthen and encourage them when their faith is wavering. People with the gift of exhortation have the ability (as the Spirit enable them) to motivate others as well as challenge and rebuke them in order to develop them spiritually. People with this gift desire to see everyone in the church remain in Christ and flourish in all spheres of life. I am humbled and do not take for granted when friends tell me they could not do what I do and I am sure I cannot do what they do either. I always thought we are all called to exhort others until I noticed it is a gift to encourage somebody. I used to complain and get angry that people do not help them the way I do to others but now I embrace everyone's gift because we are all one, serving the same master. However, it is an act of selfishness to keep our gift to ourselves or use it only to bless those we think deserve it while we receive or get blessed by other's gifts. I believe most Christians have some level of this gift as we need it in the body of Christ to support one another as we walk the journey of faith. Paul did not cease to exhort, counsel, encourage and strengthen even when he was in prison or going through hardship. He was an extraordinary person who put his life on hold to help a sister or go through a difficult journey to encourage a brother. I pray that our life and the gifts that the Holy Spirit has apportioned to us will be used to glorify God. (**See also Romans 12:8, Acts 11:23-24; 14:21-22; 15:32; 20: 1-3, 22-23).**

GIVING: This gift speaks for itself. Most believers have this gift and there are some specific people in the church that operate in the gift of giving. The Greek word for the gift of giving is **"Metadidomi" meaning to impart, give or share.** However, this word is also accompanied by another descriptive word **"Haplotes"** which tells us more about this kind of giving **(Romans 12:8)**. The word **"Haplotes"** means **to have a simple, sincere, honest and generous heart that is free from pretence or hypocrisy**. It takes a person with a gift of giving like Joseph of Arimathea to personally put the body of our Lord Jesus in his own personal tomb. He saw the need and was bold enough to approach Pilate to release the body of our Lord to him at the time when everyone was afraid of provide a place of rest for Him. His name was mentioned once in the bible but what he did was not forgotten. **As evening approached, there came a rich man from Arimathea, named Joseph, who had himself become a disciple of Jesus. Going to Pilate, he asked for Jesus' body, and Pilate ordered that it be given to him. Joseph took the body, wrapped it in a clean linen cloth, and placed it in his own new tomb that he had cut out of the rock. He rolled a big stone in front of the entrance to the tomb and went away (Matthew27:57-60).** I have heard people like Pastor Matthew Ashimolowo donate food, clothing, cars to nations, widows, pastors and most of the time the people are not necessarily related to Him. It takes an extra ordinary act of giving to provoke this kind of generosity **(Act20:35)**

The Holy Spirit gives this gift to meet the various needs in the church, ministries, missionaries and people who do not have the means to provide for themselves. I believe people with this gift love to share from their overflow of God's blessings to others. They are hospitable in sharing their home, money and time in order to help others. They are great stewards and will often adjust their lifestyles in order to give more to spread the Gospel and care for the needy. Through the book of Acts you see believers sold property and possessions to give to anyone who had a need, they shared food with sincere hearts and there were no needy people found among them. **(2 Corinthians 8:1-5; Acts 2:44-47; 4:32-37**). I cannot help myself but to stress that giving should be a culture every believer must adopt. The bible promises that those who give cheerfully will be abundantly blessed and satisfied. **(2Corinthians 9:6-14).** Our attitude towards giving will provoke a blessing **(Philippians4:14-19).** Abel's sacrifice was accepted because he brought a fat portion and the firstborn of his flocks to the Lord **(Genesis4:4).**

LEADERSHIP: The gift of leadership is similar to the gift of administration and pastor. **The Greek word** for the gift of leadership is **"Proistemi"** which simply means **to lead, guard, assist, protect and care for others.** The gift of leadership is among the gifts mentioned in **Romans 12:8.** I used to think that leadership means to lead people but having led a team and a house group in my local church, I realised it is more than that; it is about building relationships with people. I remember when I was told to lead a team/group, I did not think I had the capacity to do it but I was willing to use the gift my leader saw in me to serve faithfully. I held on to what my leader said to me to just be myself and this really helped me to grow into the role of leadership. Having said that, I have attended various leadership training/ conferences, read books on leadership, listened to messages, to understand that leadership is not about me, I am part of a team that will build a church. Even though the ability to lead was there because I was born to lead, it was when I stepped into leadership that I realised I could do it. Leadership is not as simple as I thought but I have learnt that if I want to have a group or a team, I have to lead by example and people will follow me based on what they have seen me do. I understood my role was to guard, assist, protect and care for those that God had put under me to lead. I saw leadership as serving people and in return people served me by turning up to serve their Father and contributing to the team.

In **1 Thessalonians 5:12-13,** Paul urged the brothers and sisters in Thessalonians to acknowledge those who worked hard and cared for them. He asked them to hold these people in love and highest regard because of the work they did. Also, my experience of leadership has helped me to lead effectively at my workplace. I must confess that this gift allowed me to grow deeper in my relationship with God and the Holy Spirit gave me wisdom every step of the way. Did I get everything right as a leader? No, but I learnt from my mistakes, apologised for the bad decisions I made embraced my weaknesses and strength and appreciated people with different gifts from me because we are all serving Jesus. As part of a leadership team, I was able to achieve many tasks and objectives and still cared for the well-being of others. I believe people with this gift are entrepreneurial and willing to take risks to see the kingdom of God advance through the church. They will go to great lengths to support, assist and guide those God has put under them to lead. Many times I have been able to lead while going through difficult seasons of my own (i.e. health issues, divorce and homelessness) and was still able to resolve any problems that came up among the brothers and sisters in the church, fellowship or group and community. **In 1 Timothy 3** Paul focused on what true leadership in the church should look like i.e. respectable, self-control, faithfulness in a marriage, family management, not violent, not a lover of money just to mention a few. **It is worth reading the book of Timothy and Titus to enhance your understanding of the gift of leadership.**

MERCY/KINDNESS: The gift of mercy is among the gifts mentioned in **Romans 12:8. The Greek word for mercy is "eleeo" which means to help and show compassion towards those who are weak and afflicted.** The gift of mercy covers the physical, emotional, spiritual and psychological wellbeing of those in need **(Matthew 25:31-40).** God is merciful and as children of God we ought to be merciful to those around us **(Ephesians 2:4-5).** Jesus taught us to be merciful, when He told the story of a king who called his slaves to settle accounts with them and how he pardoned the one who owed him the most but the slave he pardoned refused to have mercy on his fellow slave who owed little compared to how much he owed the King **(Matthew 18:33).** I believe people with this gift, have great empathy for others and are able to come alongside people and help them as they go through their struggles which many times include the process of healing and recovery. I have received this kindness from people when I needed someone to babysit my kids, when I needed someone to walk with me through my sickness and recovery journey, included me in their family when I had no one to support me and clothed me when I needed a change of wardrobe. Majority of these people are not my relatives or people who speak my mother's tongue, they are just believers like you and I fulfilling their duty in the body of Christ. I often say that the people I met in church are more available to render support to me more than my family. I believe everyone associated with Christ should be able to show mercy as Christ showed mercy to us and died for the sins He did not commit. **The bible says while we were yet a sinner Christ died for us (Romans 5:6-8).** God sent His only son to die for our sins even though the world rejected Him. His desire is that no one will perish but that we will have everlasting life.

My pastor (Gary Clark) will do anything to help the poor. In his siege to do more than just giving money to the homeless, the Greenlight project came to existence. Greenlight is a group of people (medics, doctors, nurses, carers) who go out on the streets of London to provide medical support the homeless as well as chat with them. From this, many homeless people have received medical support they are not entitled to; they have been able to move into their own accommodation with the support of other partnerships and even provided jobs for many. People with this gift do not just think about themselves but carry other peoples' burdens on their shoulders. The gift of mercy helps to strengthen the people of God and assists those who are suffering. People with this gift are able to weep with those who weep **(Romans 12:15)** and bear other's burden **(Galatians 6:2).** Some of the qualities I have seen the people with this gift possess are their sensitivity to the feelings of others, their discernment when things are not going well with people, their heart simplicity and their willingness to be there for people. They are happy to leave their own problems behind in order to come alongside someone who is hurting. They are good listeners and are willing to sacrifice their time, resources and money to support the needs of others. (**See other scriptures that talked about the gift of Mercy/ Kindness: Matthew 5:7, Luke 10:30-37, Galatians5:22, Ephesians4:32, James 3:17, Act20:35).**

PASTOR: The **Greek word** for pastor is **"poimen"** which means shepherd or overseer. The word **Pastor (ro'eh) in Hebrew** means to feed/tend to. In **John21,** Jesus told Peter to feed the people three times even though Peter did not know or understand why He emphasised the word several times: **When they had finished eating, Jesus said to Simon Peter, "Simon son of John, do you love me more than these?" "Yes, Lord," he said, "you know that I love you." Jesus said, "Feed my lambs." Again Jesus said, "Simon son of John, do you love me?" He answered, "Yes, Lord, you know that I love you." Jesus said, "Take care of my sheep." The third time he said to him, "Simon son of John, do you love me?" Peter was hurt because Jesus asked him the third time, "Do you love me?" He said,**

"Lord, you know all things; you know that I love you." Jesus said, "Feed my sheep (verse15-17). Pastors have the ability to do many things and operate in other gifts such as leadership, teaching, service, prophetic, healing, apostleship. The responsibilities of the pastor are similar to that of shepherds who look after sheep. They feed everyone who walks into the church with the word of God, protect and care for the wounded and nurse them back to health. I believe pastors have the knowledge and understanding of the scriptures and are able to encourage and admonish the church with sound doctrine.

People with this gift have the ability to teach the scriptures and oversee the running of the church at the same time. There are some qualities of a pastor that Paul instructed Titus to follow in Titus1: **An elder must be blameless, faithful to his wife, a man whose children believe and are not open to the charge of being wild and disobedient. Since an overseer manages God's household, he must be blameless not overbearing, not quick-tempered, not given to drunkenness, not violent, not pursuing dishonest gain. Rather, he must be hospitable, one who loves what is good, who is self-controlled, upright, holy and disciplined. 9He must hold firmly to the trustworthy message as it has been taught, so that he can encourage others by sound doctrine and refute those who oppose it (Titus 1:6-9).** Pastors are called to serve the people just like the shepherds serve their sheep. Paul urged the people of Ephesus to live a life worthy of what they were called to do i.e. be completely humble, gentle and patient. These qualities and more are needed in order for pastors to equip the people for the work of the ministry, strengthen their faith and help them mature **(Ephesian 4: 2, 11).** The fact that you are called by God does not mean that you have everything you need to pastor a church. Work with the Holy Spirit to help and show you what you need and how to pastor His people in His way for He knows them better than you do. Pastors are able to share tears with those who are down **(Romans 12:15)** and bear their burdens **(Galatians 6:2).** My pastor (Gary Clark) is the perfect example of this gift; he puts himself in someone else's shoes. He decided to put funds aside to help solo parents simply because he felt that if two people do struggle to look after two children how much more for a solo parent? My children and I benefited from this generosity when we were made homeless and when we moved to our new flat. We are so thankful to pastor Gary. Most pastors tend to show this gift through their love, patience, compassion and kindness towards others. They tend to be good listeners and there is nothing anyone can do to stop them from helping others even to the detriment of their own soul.

SERVICE: The gift of service is given to help the church and the community **(1 Corinthians 12:28).** Most believers operate in this gift. They are people who organise things in the church and make sure the church runs well by ensuring that the church staff are paid, flowers are delivered for the Sunday service etc. They are volunteers who serve every Sunday, at conferences and meetings. However, there are some people who are exceptionally given this gift by the Holy Spirit: **Jesus called them together and said, "You know that those who are regarded as rulers of the Gentiles lord it over them, and their high officials exercise authority over them. Not so with you. Instead, whoever wants to become great among you must be your servant, and whoever wants to be first must be slave of all. For even the Son of Man did not come to be served, but to serve, and to give his life as a ransom for many." (Mark10:42-45).** People with this gift fill many gaps in the ministry that most people with other gifts cannot. They serve the church so that others in the body of Christ with other spiritual gifts (pastors, leaders) can concentrate on what the Lord has commissioned them to do and use their gifts to the fullest. The gift of service is a commitment to serve in any capacity and those with this gift are content to serve anywhere to build the church and they do it generously with a free will **(2 Corinthians 9:6-7).** They do not only serve in a local church but are active in the community, hence spreading the Gospel and helping others to find their faith. They are the kind of people that will arrive first before everyone and last to leave. They do not seem to be tired of serving others and are content with who they are. While others want to own their own business or ministry, they are convinced that they are called to serve alongside or under someone and they do it well. They are very loyal, disciplined and protective over those they serve.

There is a couple that I know with this amazing gift of serving. Eugene and Angela have been so kind to my family in so many ways. They keep my family in mind when they are doing their own shopping. When they are going to the butchers, Ikea or Costco, they will ask for our shopping list and deliver it to our house because I do not drive. They hosted sleep overs for my boys when they were young. They will go out of their way to help and support us. Recently, I did a recording through anchor "My journey to 48" and I asked Angela in an interview as to why they supported us the way they did despite the fact that they did not know us then. In a humble spirit she said; "we just did what we could to help". When I started the elderly project, they did not only support me financially but they made it possible. They are both a gift sent to me. People with this gift do not seek recognition or a position but they just want to help wherever needed. Their contributions do not only bless the church but everyone around them, showing the love of Christ to the world and bring glory to God. What Angela and Eugene did for me, I will never forget. They showed me how to treat others and helped me to recognise the needs around me **(Act9:39-43).** Their generosity and their acts of service propelled me to serve two elderly homes in Dagenham. They reminded me of the apostle and the people that worked alongside them. People like Timothy, Titus, joseph (a Levite from Cyprus), Joseph from Arimathea, Cornelius (a centurion from Caesarea) and Mark. **(Acts 4:36-37, Act 6:1-7, Luke 10:30-37, 2 Timothy 4:11, Revelation 2:19)**

TEACHING: The gift of teaching is given by the Holy Spirit to help others understand the word of God better. Jesus came to teach the truth about His Father and even though they were resistant to His teaching as it was not what the people wanted to hear, He kept teaching the truth. Without the true revelation of the word of God, people will wander from faith, go astray and sin against the Lord their God **(Proverbs 29:18). This gift is given to enhance the growth and maturity of the people.**

In my understanding, people with the gift of teaching love to study the word of God. They read other material; use what is going on around them and whatever is available to them to express the word of God. They spend time in God's presence in order to receive revelation from the Holy Spirit on what to talk about and issues to address in the body of Christ. Anyone can teach the word of God but only words instructed by the Holy Spirit can bring deliverance and salvation. Those people with this gift have the ability to effectively communicate the word of God in a way that believers and non-believers will understand. Jesus was our greatest example of the gift of teaching. People always gathered around to hear Him teach and sometimes refused to leave in the process and He had to sneak out of the crowd **(Luke 4:30-32**). Jesus's teaching touched and influenced everyone who heard him. Prominent people like scholars of the word **(Luke10:25)** and Jewish leaders came to Jesus to be taught by Him **(Matthew15:1).** He was calm, humbled and patient when answering their questions. Signs and wonders followed Him as He expanded the word of God **(John 4:6).** He was never tired of teaching the word of His Father; no wonder crowds followed Him wherever He went.

I believe a teacher must be knowledgeable, willing to learn and above all rely on the Holy Spirit to deliver the message God has put on their heart. Many times in the bible the apostles were moved by the spirit and were able to speak with boldness (Check the book of Acts).Teachers of the word of God take great joy in seeing that others learn and apply the truth of God's word into their lives. They are able to demonstrate God's love and reveal His truth to the world without fear. Going to bible school is not a license to becoming a great teacher but it will give insight into the deeper revelation about the bible. There are many great inspirational speakers but not all have the effect of setting people free. Paul told us to teach if we are called to teach for it is by God's grace that we can do what we do, not by power or might but by the Spirit so that no one can boast. **For by the grace given me I say to every one of you: Do not think of yourself more highly than you ought, but rather think of yourself with sober judgment, in accordance with the faith God has distributed to each of you. For just as each of us has one body with many members, and these members do not all have the same function, so in Christ we, though many, form one body, and each member belongs to all the others. We have different gifts, according to the grace given to each of us. If your gift is prophesying, then prophesy in accordance with your faith; if it is serving, then serve; if it is teaching, then teach; if it is to encourage, then give encouragement; if it is giving, then give generously; if it is to lead, do it diligently; if it is to show mercy, do it cheerfully (Romans12:3-8) .**

I need to clarify that it is not necessarily that a pastor is a good communicator of the word of God, some pastors are put in the position because no one is willing to do it or because their husband/wife is a pastor or because they are leaders. And because you are a teacher of the word of God does not mean you have what it takes to pastor a church. Understand your call and stay within what the Holy Spirit will enable you to do. However, there would be times where you have to step in to help a ministerial gift. Most people with the gift of administration, mercy, prophetic, serving and exhortation tend to teach in the capacity the Holy Spirit enables them. Moses was a leader but Aaron was the one who communicated to the people about whatever God said to Moses. Jesus was a teacher that is why he was called a rabbi and people were amazed by His teaching. When it came to welfare, the disciples catered for that. He told them where to get a cot for free, where to eat and the disciples made it happen. So, stay within your calling. When I was a group/team leader, was I a teacher? No, but I shared the word of God based on my knowledge and time spent in God's presence.

I believe that you have been blessed with the revelation of each gift. There are other gifts that are not mentioned in this chapter but there are many resources out there if you are interested to learn more.

PRAYER AND CONFESSION

Father, we are grateful for the spiritual gifts You have given the church.

It is a privilege and honour to serve others with this precious gift

Thank You for the grace to teach Your word in the way that people will understand and expand the kingdom in order to point people to Christ

Thank You Holy Spirit for the gift of administration

We are grateful for the gift of apostleship

It is an honour to share the gospel to those who do not believe

Thank God for the gift of exhortation

Thank God for the gift of mercy and kindness

It is a privilege to lead the people of God

Thank You Holy Spirit for the spiritual gift of discernment

Thank You Holy Spirit for the interpretations in our bible studies

Thank You God for revealing Your heart through the gift of prophesy

We give You the glory for the gift to pastors in churches

Lord, I am grateful for the spiritual gift of the word of wisdom and special knowledge in our connect groups/ fellowships

What a privilege to be able to speak in tongues

We are grateful for the spiritual gift of healing in our meetings

We appreciate Your spiritual gift of miracles and miraculous powers

We recognise Your spiritual gift of faith in our services

As individuals and as a cooperate body we say thank You Holy spirit for the gifts You have given us to edify the church, bring growth and maturity, build the church, reveal who You are, bring clarity and revelation of Your word, show the world You are God and You love them, to trust in You and communicate with You

May we use this gift to glorify the name of the Lord not ourselves.

These are not just gifts but a reminder that You love us and You want to have a relationship with us, so we say thank You sir.

MAN

It's a boy!

Blue ribbons, balloons, pictures and flowers are commonly displayed or given to the parents few days after a child is born. The cute baby will start his journey to adulthood by going through seasons i.e. lots of fun, crying, laughter, mood swings, tantrums, crawling and walking. Even for a new born, God's intention for his life does not change. He has been given authority over the things that God made. The prognosis for this little boy is to become a man. **So God created man in his own image, in the image and likeness of God He created him; male and female he created them .And God blessed them and said to them [granting them certain authority] and said to them, "Be fruitful, multiply and fill the earth, and subjugate it [putting it under your power]; and rule over (dominate) the fish of the sea, the birds of the air, and every living things that moves upon the earth." (Genesis1: 27-28AMP).** The bible does not tell us why a man was made first instead of a boy. I guess it is a mystery that only God can clarify. In the world, production starts from conception and then a child is born. Even Jesus was born. What makes this man Adam different to the rest of us? It is a metaphor. The law of gravity dictates that when you throw something up it must come down, what happens in between is unknown. When a male child is born, a man is born. God is not thinking about how this child is going to become a man. He already sees the end before the beginning. The way mankind thinks and reason is different from the way God thinks.

"For my thoughts are not your thoughts, neither are your ways my way," declares the Lord. "As the heavens are higher than the earth, so are my ways higher than your ways and my thoughts than your thoughts."(Isaiah 55:8-9)

When my boys were born I sought the face of the Lord to know about the character of each child. The revelation may not be accurate or fully understood in reality, but it prepared me for the challenges that came later. I am constantly reminded of God's promise and an assurance that it will be well with both my sons. Rebekah was concerned when the twin babies in her womb began to struggle with each other and she inquired of the Lord: **When she inquires of the Lord, the Lord said, "Two nations are in your womb, two peoples shall be separated from your body; One people shall be stronger than the other, And the older shall serve the younger"(Genesis25:23).** However, Rebekah's effort to help God to bring the promise to pass on the basis of her own understanding of what she was told resulted in separation and anger. Her husband's **(Isaac)** interference ended up in rebellion, bitterness and resentment. **(Genesis27)** God is the only one who knows everything. Do not try to help God. Jeremiah said: **The word of the Lord came to him, saying, "Before I formed you in the womb I knew you, before you were born I set you apart; I appointed you as a prophets to the nation"(Jeremiah1:4-5).** The Lord knows the end before the beginning. That is why He is the Alpha and the Omega, the Beginning and the End.

As this child begins to grow and learn about the world, he will soon realise he cannot be a baby forever. Bills have to be paid, he is given responsibilities, decisions and choices have to be made. BOOM! Life is tough and exciting at the same time. Graduation, great friendships, broken relationships, work, disappointment, failure, success and more responsibilities become more of a reality than fiction. A question like what is my purpose in life in all of this starts coming up. So what happened to that child? He grew up! While some men literally take God at His word and become great leaders / rulers, be fruitful and multiply, some men have a tough time being themselves due to so many reasons. Reasons caused by others or by themselves, beliefs that are not true and lies that override God's promises for mankind are some of the reasons people fail to rise to the plan God has for their life.

And another reason of course is generational curses which we will come to in a while. But firstly let me share some of the things some men have told me about the reason why they were not able to activate that promise that has already been deposited in their life. They believe the lie that 'women are favoured more than men' or 'women are evil' or ' the world is a world of a woman', or they are disadvantaged because they were born in a certain part of the world, discriminated because they are black/ a man, they had no role model growing up, they were raised by a single mother or their father was absent, it's the curse placed on them by God **(Genesis 3:11-19),** it is not easy to be a man, it is the devil's fault. Perhaps, it is the curse placed on Cain, which they forgot to read the part where the Lord put a mark on Cain so that anyone who found him would not kill him and on top of that, he was able to build a city **(Genesis 4:15&17)**. As much as some of these issues/ beliefs may be so real, the choice still lies solely on an individual. The power of free choice is paramount; choose today to be that man that God created you to be. The image and likeness of God.

Let us go back to the beginning, man was given responsibilities to work, take care of the Garden of Eden (just to recap) and whatever man called something so it was. It is really sad that some men in our society have sold their birth right to circumstances surrounding them and have refused to step into that responsibility that God had given them. I may be wrong as I am writing from a woman's point of view but this is what some men have told me are the issues standing in their way of success. Having said all this, some men have also misused their authority and become egocentric and power driven. This trait first came about when mankind thought they can hide from God when they ate from the tree God commanded them not to eat but instead of being remorseful Adam and Eve blamed each other **(Genesis3)**. Men and women were both given responsibilities to rule, be fruitful and multiply. However, each person has reasons why they are who they are. Women are born to be helpers, men are born to lead. **Adam named his wife Eve, because she would become the mother of all the living. (Genesis 3:20 NIV)**.

At no point in creation did man say he could not do the tasks God gave mankind to do. Adam was faithful and hardworking but was not even looking for a helper, it was God who saw that He needed a helper. You are created to be a man with power and authority to rule and dominate the earth. I am not talking about men who beat their wives because they want to teach them to submit to authority. Those men are literally hurting themselves and they don't realise that they were created in the image of God and God is love. A man who hurts his fellow brother or sister does not love God and he is not a believer. **If someone says, "I love God," and hates his brother, he is a liar; for he who does not love his brother whom he has seen, how can he love God whom he has not seen? And this commandment we have from Him: that he who loves God must love his brother also. (1John4:20-21). Beloved, let us love one another, for love is of God; and everyone who loves is born of God and knows God. He who does not love does not know God, for God is love. (1 John 4:7-8.)**

It's never too late to start doing what is right. Age is not a limit. You can become great at any age but it is important to do what is right before the Lord because that is what makes a difference. I want to mention a few people in the bible that made an impact at different ages in life. Some of them did it in their own way and it cost them dearly but those who put God at the centre of everything produced good results. Do not limit what God can do at any age of your life. **Samuel** was just a boy when he started ministering and the Lord spoke to him even though it was rare in those days **(1Samuel3). Rehoboam** was 41 years old when he began to reign and reigned for 17years. He acted foolishly by rejecting the advice of the elders and consulting the young men who gave him wrong advice and all Israelites turned away from him. He could have had both the house of Judah and Israel **(1King12)**. Abijah was 18 years of age when he became King of Judah and he only reigned for 3 years because he continued the evil deeds his father Jeroboam committed in his days **(1Kings15)**. **Asa** was 20 years of age when he became King of Judah and he reigned 41 years by doing what was right in the sight of God **(1Kings15)**.

Joash was 7years old when he became king. His story was remarkable. When a king's mother **(Athaliah)** found out that her son was dead, she decided to kill the whole royal family but the sister of the king who died, stole **Joash** from the royal princess and hid him away from the murderer **(2 Kings11&12)**. **Joash** did what was right in the eyes of God and he reigned for 40 years in Jerusalem. You might be thinking; 'that was in the Old Testament'. Let us look at New Testament. **Jesus** was 12 years old when he sat among teachers at the temple courts listening and asking questions. And all who heard Him could not believe His understanding and how He answered questions. **(Luke 2:41-50)**. Jesus started His ministry at the age of 30 years old and by the theory of bible scholar His ministry lasted 3 years **(Luke 3:23)**. Zechariah, John the Baptist's father was speechless from the day he received the revelation that his wife Elizabeth will conceive until the day of the naming of his son. With or without his belief God fulfilled His promise **(Luke1)**. No matter how old you are, God's promises for your life do not change.

Now let's look at the curses some men always refer to when things do not go well in their life. What is a curse? Merriam-Webster states: 'a prayer or invocation for harm or injury to come upon one, a profane or obscene oath or word, something that is cursed or accursed'. **Christ has redeemed us from the curse of the law, having become a curse for us (for it is written, "Cursed is everyone who hangs on a tree"), that the blessing of Abraham might come upon the Gentiles in Christ, that we might receive the promise of the Spirit through faith (Galatians 3:13-14 NKJV).** If you are a child of God you are no longer under the curse, you are free. Jesus took our curse on the cross so that we can receive the promises of life. Why then do people believe that we are under the curse? That is the lie of the devil to keep us bound and in captive but we are redeemed from the law. We are no longer under the law, we are free indeed. If you did wrong, repent and ask the Father to forgive you and He will. According to the law in the Old Testament only Jewish people can come to God but when Jesus died on the cross the veil in the temple tore from top to bottom **(Matthew27:51)** making it possible for people like you and I to come to God's presence, we do not need the priest to carry our sacrifice to God, Jesus did all that for us. The body of Jesus broken for us predestined us for adoption to sonship, the blood He shed forgave our sins and brought unity between heaven and earth, His death gave us a guaranteed inheritance **(Ephesians1).**

If you base your belief on what happened in Genesis (the book of the beginning) you will miss out on all the other things that happened in the rest of the book. If you remain stuck in the beginning, how will you fulfil the promises God promised you at the end? There is a saying that; everything that starts has to end. Even Adam and Eve who were cursed moved forward to produce, increase, multiply and be fruitful. The fall of man does not mean the end of man. If you find yourself at the bottom get back up. Refuse to give the enemy of your soul something to rejoice about. You cannot just stay in the beginning and not move forward. If you hold on to the curse placed on Adam then what Jesus did for you is useless. God told Joshua; "my servant Moses is dead move forward and possess the land promised to your fore fathers" **(Joshua 1:6).** The Lord told Abram to leave his country and his family to the land He will show him. If Abram had refused, He will not be called the father of faith today **(Genesis 12-13). Noah** was told to build an ark because the world was going to be destroyed, if he had refused to build the ark he would have perished with the rest of the people who died **(Genesis 7-9).** Do not allow what someone has done to you or how tough your journey of life has been to determine how your future will be. Jesus told someone to go and wash at the pool, if he had refused to go his condition would have remained with him **(John 9:1-7).** If you are not in a good place, ask God to show you what to do next, retrace your steps back to when things started going wrong in your life and ask God to guide you.

A lot of people do not like to do a self- assessment of themselves because of fear of what they might find out. Years ago, I was prompted by the Holy Spirit to revaluate my finance. I consider myself a good steward of my spending but unwillingly with fear and trembling I yielded to the voice of God because I knew it is for my own good and I have realised that when God does something in my life, it starts by shedding off some bad habits. Anyway, I would like to tell you that I was indeed a good steward but that is not what happened. I was shocked to find out that I had direct debits that I had set up for years and they were not bringing any benefit to my life. By the time I cut down on foolish spending as proverbs calls it, I was amazed at how much I had left and still able to tithe, save and be a blessing. Before I started evaluating my finances I was telling God that I do not have money to do all that I have to do but by the time I finished I realised I have more than enough. So, do not give up on that dream yet, do not give up on yourself yet, there is still hope as long as you are breathing. A person who decides to end their life believe that life is over and cannot see past where they are, I pray that will not be your portion.

The account in Genesis that brought the downfall to mankind was redeemed by Jesus when He died on the cross. The bible says while we were yet sinners Christ died for us. You do not have to carry any more curse or bondage around with you. It died when Jesus died on the Cross. Why then do men bring up this curse whenever things are not going well in their life? **To Adam He said, "Because you listened to your wife and ate fruit from the tree about which I commanded you, 'You must not eat from it,' "Cursed is the ground because of you; through painful toil you will eat food from it all the days of your life. It will produce thorns and thistles for you, and you will eat the plants of the field. By the** sweat of your brow you will eat your food until you return to the ground, since for us from it you were taken; for dust you are and to dust you will return." (Genesis3:17-19). Adam received these consequences and passed them down to generations to come after him (including us) because he disobeyed God. But for those who believe in Christ, repent of their sins, ask for God's forgiveness and accept Christ as their Lord and saviour the curse has been reversed to blessing when Jesus died. That is what happened when you got baptised, when you go in water you die with Christ and when you rise up, you are raised with Christ **"Or don't you know that all of us who were baptized into Christ Jesus were baptized into his death? We were therefore buried with him through baptism into death in order that, just as Christ was raised from the dead through the glory of the Father, we too may live a new life (Romans6:3-4).** You are born to be fruitful, multiply, replenish and subdue the earth.

Circumstances that surround you do not replace this blessing in your life. A child born premature or with physical difficulties does not stop God's love for the child. Ros Blackburn was diagnosed with autism at the age of one but became a trainer helping people with autism to understand who they are and she also helped staff who work with autistic kids to know how to relate with their service users. Was Ros cured of her autism? No, but her experience, weaknesses and strength have helped many. All odds were against her but she did not let it affect who she is. As a believer, she understood she was born for this time like this. Listening to her years ago talked about her life and her difficulties made me realise that God is no respecter of person. If you have no eyes, God can use it for His glory. I liked it when she said that "humans like to control things but she likes her life because she does not have to do anything she does not want to do". To us we see her as been unfortunate because she is autistic but she sees it as "an opportunity to be who she want to be without being forced to marry or go to university" **(Ros Blackburn 15/9/2016).**

Having said this I need to clarify that there is are consequences when we disobey God especially, when we refuse to repent from our sins. The best thing to do when we disobey God is to repent and not bring judgement on ourselves. Our Father is merciful and compassionate. At the age of 15 when I decided to walk away from God and ended up being abused, was this God's fault or judgement? No, I chose to walk away from God's protection hence I exposed myself to danger. Was God there with me? Yes, of course, if He was not I would have been consumed by life and messed up my future. The devil is the one that infiltrates suffering and pain to make it look like our Father does not love us or He is punishing us. The Lord loves us so much that He gave His son to die for us and His son brought us abundant life. His blessings bring riches and add no sorrow **(Proverbs10:22KJV).** When you fall, get up. It does not matter how many times you fall, it just makes you stronger. Do not give up and do not give in to failure. Refuse to be identified by your circumstances, you are better than that. You say 'I have been treated with injustice and the system has not worked in my favour', I sympathize with you and pray that God will restore everything the enemy has taken from you and comfort you. But I also want you to use that energy to exercise on integrity, prudence, hard-work, truth and kindness. This will pay off one day.

Many people have been affected by injustice and treated unfairly in our society and only God can change the heart of men and bring a change into our society. If you are on the receiving end of human wickedness, I will advise you to allow the Lord to fight your battle and do what looks impossible for you to do. To be honest with you, the situation becomes interesting when your Father intervenes. Do not waste your energy on a fight you are unable to win by your power. Do not allow yourself to be consumed by hatred, revenge, anger, un-forgiveness, bitterness or resentment that you lose your worth in the process. **Consider it pure joy, my brothers and sisters, whenever you face trials of many kinds, because you know that the testing of your faith produces perseverance. Let perseverance finish its work so that you may be mature and complete, not lacking anything. If any of you lacks wisdom, you should ask God, who gives generously to all without finding fault, and it will be given to you. But when you ask, you must believe and not doubt, because the one who doubts is like a wave of the sea, blown and tossed by the wind. (James 1:3-6).** I am so intrigued by Richard Branson story. A dyslexia school dropout at 16, now an entrepreneur who is worth billions. Trust God that all things are possible.

PRAYER AND CONFESSION

I am who God says I am. I am a child of God

I am no longer a slave to fear and failure. He that the son of God set free is free indeed. I am a man created in God's image and likeness.

I will listen to Godly advice. O Lord, Give me wisdom like Solomon that caused the whole world to come to him and bless him. Solomon's intelligence attracted wealth, may my intellect and talent attract wealth, prestige and recognition. May my wealth attract people to the Almighty God.

I will be fruitful in the land. I will flourish and multiply. I will not be a man who neglects his duty but God's image will be seen in me and through me everywhere I go. I will not be jealous of my brother and sister that I plan evil against them

Search my heart God and find nothing filthy in me. Remove every blemish that is blocking my miracle. Create in me a clean heart and renew a right spirit within me. Remove every filthy habit and behaviour that dishonour you in my life. Let no evil come out of my mouth

Let me embrace what you are doing in my life and not allow un-forgiveness, resentment and bitterness to destroy my life.

I am a man respected by neighbours, my family and friends, employer and employee. A man that will hold his birth right as a precious gift. A man that will not compromise his belief because of fame, wealth and greed

I am blessed and not cursed. I have been redeemed from the curse of the law for cursed are those hang on the tree for the blessing of Abraham is mine.

When things are not going well in my life, I will not automatically assume it is because I am cursed but search that my heart is pure and holy before Him and believe my time to receive my breakthrough will come.

I take authority on those things that are tormenting my soul. Distractions and disturbances that want to steal my joy, kill my dreams and destroy my faith. I depart from every works of unrighteousness and impurities. I declare I am free because who the Lord set free is free in deed.

Jazeb cried out to the God of Israel, Oh that you would bless me and enlarge my territory! Let your hands be with me, and keep me from harm so that I will be free from pain", And God granted his request. **(1 Chronicles 4:9-10)**

I cry unto You today, I do not know what curses have been inflated on me from birth or passed from one generation to generation but as Jabez, I cry out to You; deliver me and bless me. Enlarge my territory that my forefathers have hindered due to ignorance. Place Your hands on me and keep me from harm. As You oh God had granted Jabez's requests, grant my request today in Jesus's name.

(Esther3-7) Every plan that was meant against me the Lord will turn it around to bless me. Arise oh Lord, let the enemy that wants to destroy my body, soul and spirit not succeed. Heaven arise and destroy every evil activity over my life and children. Lift your standard against anything that has risen its head above You in my life. I silence every scheme and plan of the enemy.

I raise Halleluyah over fear, doubt, unfinished projects, lack, sickness, laziness and lack of discipline. I put on truth, righteousness, word of God, praise, thanksgiving, faith and the willingness to serve God in any capacity.

HOMOSEXUALITY

The Lord God said, "It is not good for the man to be alone. I will make a helper suitable for him." Then the Lord God made a woman from the rib he had taken out of the man, and he brought her to the man. The man said, "This is now bone of my bones and flesh of my flesh; she shall be called 'woman,' for she was taken out of man." That is why a man leaves his father and mother and is united to his wife, and they become one flesh. Adam and his wife were both naked, and they felt no shame. (Genesis 2:18, 22-25). I do understand that this chapter may be awkward and sensitive to my readers. My intention is not to upset you but to bring awareness to a subject that is often not mentioned in Christianity but it is a hidden practiced. I do not have a desire to become homosexual and I am not a lesbian but I have colleagues and neighbours who are gay and lesbians. I am not an expert on the subject nor a bible scholar but the Spirit of truth will reveal the Father's heart concerning the matter and above all give understanding to those reading this book.

According to the scriptures above, God's intention was for a man and woman to join together in a holy matrimony. My belief is if God wanted a man to man relationship, He would not have created a woman, He would have created another man. This is a debate to reserve for God when we see Him face to face but while on earth let us concentrate on who God is and His intentions for the mankind He created. God is love and everyone who loves God has been made complete through Jesus Christ who lives in us. The love that God shows to humanity is without conditions, whether we deserve it or not, His son sacrificed His life for us. The love that God offers humanity does not envy or boast or dishonour others or self-seeking. God's love does not keep a record of wrongs, or gets easily angered. His love delights not in evil but protects us from evil. God's Love is patient, kind, hopeful, truthful and perseveres to the end **(1Corinthians 13; 1 John 4)**. As we look into this subject, it is important to ask ourselves what is God's opinion on this? What does the spirit of truth say regarding the matter? Do we love others? Are we willing to allow someone to dishonour God because of our feelings? What are our views about the following: prostitution, modern slavery, human trafficking, adultery, pornography, rape, exotic dance, nakedness (as in what you wear); showing the world what was meant to be kept private. If you do not see any issue with this then it will be difficult for you to see homosexuality as a sin. Why do I believe homosexuality is a sin? **We know that the law is good if one uses it properly. We also know that the law is made not for the righteous but for lawbreakers and rebels, the ungodly and sinful, the unholy and irreligious, for those who kill their fathers or mothers, for murderers, for the sexually immoral, for those practicing homosexuality, for slave traders and liars and perjurers—and for whatever else is contrary to the sound doctrine that conforms to the gospel concerning the glory of the blessed God, which he entrusted to me (1Timothy 1:8-11).**

According to scriptures homosexuality is not different from committing sexual immorality, worshipping other gods, having sexual intercourse with someone else apart from the spouse, being greedy, theft, drunkards, swindlers and slanders **(1 Corinthians6:9-20; Romans 1:26–32).** Homosexuality/pansexuality (pansexuality means that you're attracted to people of all genders) is not how God made or sees mankind. If a man is born a man why does he need to change his gender? Change of gender or behaving a certain way doesn't make you less a man or more of a woman. What you came with from heaven is who you are, do not let the devil deceive you or the society tell you who you are. God loves the way He created man and woman and everyone will give an account to God on how they have spent their life on earth. I have heard that a child can be born having the male and female features but who decides this, the doctor? Planned Parenthood talks about Intersex which is a general term used when a person is born with reproductive or sexual anatomy that doesn't fit the physical appearance of "female" or "male." Others might be identified as intersex from birth and sometimes, others might not know they're intersex until later in life, like when they go through puberty.

I believe this is straight forward without mankind interference. If a person has a womb then she is a woman. I do not know why this is confusing for humanity. God was not confused when He made Adam and Eve. I empathize that doctors have ruined people's perceptions because of their belief of what is normal or not. For those who fall in this category, I pray that God will heal and restore what has been stolen from you. Doctors are human beings just like you and I, they are not God. God loves you from when you are conceived, He said **"Before I formed you in the womb I knew you, before you were born I set you apart; I appointed you as a prophet to the nations."(Jeremiah1:5).** Do not allow what man says destroy who God created you to be. He has the final say about your life not men. I was advised by the doctor to terminate both my pregnancies because my ex-husband and I have an AS blood type but we believed God's promises and none of my sons have sickle cell. Doctors are like hands of the porter that make the clay, God is the porter and the clay is the patient.

Do not get me wrong, I love doctors, I believe and appreciate what they do. Without doctors and nurses, I believe many of us would have died. The difficult cases they solve every day and the relief on their faces when a patient pulls through to life or when medical research is successful is all amazing. I have friends who are doctors, nurses and psychologists. It is important to know that the profession is a gift from God to bless humanity. However, we have become a generation that depends on doctors and medication to survive. We work ourselves till we burn out and believe that painkillers are the solution to constant headaches and tiredness. We will rather pay for medication rather than eat and sleep well. Our body is powerful, designed by God with an immune system to protect us but we have suppressed it by medication and drugs. I love it when doctors acknowledge that it is not their knowledge or intellectual that enables them to perform successful surgeries but God. Doctors are there to do their job but they are not the saviour. I have seen and heard of stories where doctors turn out to be evil, they see themselves as god and believe they have the power to heal people. In 2015 Dr Farid Fata was sentenced to 45 years in prison for misdiagnosing patients. Breasts surgeon Ian Paterson was jailed for 15 years for carrying needless operations. As Christians we need to open our eyes and discern what is going on around us and what we allow into our body. I believe there are things even professionals do not know. There are riddles and mysteries only God can reveal to mankind. When I was diagnosed with lupus, I depended on the doctors and nurses to tell me what to/not do. As I was praying for healing one day, I heard the Lord say to me to trust Him. The doctor told me that the medication I was taking was for life but the Lord disagreed and with the help of the Holy Spirit, I was able to come off the medication. Who do you believe? Is there anything too difficult that God cannot do?

God's love for mankind does not mean He will compromise His principles to suit mankind desires. When you sit for an exam, you either pass or fail, there is no in-between. It is the same with God, you cannot say you follow Christ and neglect or ignore His commands. God hates sin and the act of men having sex with another man pollutes His presence. The bible is very clear when it comes to homosexuality relationships (**Leviticus 18:22-30, 20:13, 15, 16**). It is an abomination and it defiles humanity and the land. I have an imagination of what it means to defile the presence of God and always remember it anytime a sinful nature comes to my mind - there was a big feast to mark an occasion. When it was time to eat, a swan of pigeons invaded the food, ate what they could and left their droppings making it impossible for anyone to eat the delicacies that had been prepared. Believers need to be careful not to fall for the lies and deceit of the enemy. Like I said before in the book, the main aim of the devil is to turn us away from God and he will use anything to achieve his purpose. Feelings and emotions come and go, man and woman will be born and die but the word of God remains the same. Heaven and earth will pass away, but His words will never pass away. **"Be careful, or your hearts will be weighed down with carousing, drunkenness and the anxieties of life, and that day will close on you suddenly like a trap. For it will come on all those who live on the face of the whole earth. Be always on the watch, and pray that you may be able to escape all that is about to happen, and that you may be able to stand before the Son of Man."** **(Luke21:33-36).** Do not bring a curse or judgement upon yourself.

God is Holy and wherever He is, is Holy. Our body is the temple of God and it must honour and glorify the one who owns our soul. When the people saw the lightning, thunder, smoky mountains, they removed themselves and stood far away and told Moses to speak to them instead of God speaking to them **(Exodus20:18-19).** The promiscuous life of the people of Sodom and Gomorrah brought their destruction, resulting into the whole generation being wiped out from the face of the earth. Abraham could not find ten people who were righteous in the land and even Lot could not convince the men of the land not to do evil **(Genesis 19:1–11 AMPC)**. The hearts of the people were hardened and lost in sin that they could not even see righteousness when it was presented to them. You might be thinking; but that was in the Old Testament. The old and the New Testament makes the bible complete. You cannot believe the new without the old. The prophets in the Old Testament prophesied about Jesus and the Holy Spirit. The Jesus that people believed was coming did come but they did not recognise Him because He did not look like the messiah they were expecting. Does this sound familiar? It is like history repeating itself. Human beings think they are better than God and always want to undo that which God has done such as, when a baby is born and the doctors decided what the baby should be or should not be just because he or she does not fall into the world definition of normal. Do not be fooled by the teaching that grace is sufficient even when you live in immorality. **Paul said: "What shall we say, then? Shall we go on sinning so that grace may increase? By no means! We are those who have died to sin; how can we live in it any longer? Or don't you know that all of us who were baptized into Christ Jesus were baptized into his death? We were therefore buried with him through baptism into death in order that, just as Christ was raised from the dead through the glory of the Father, we too may live a new life" (Romans6:1-4).**

We live in a different time in history where the truth has become a lie and the lie the truth. For a person who sees a ghost, that ghost is real until the ghost disappears and cannot be seen by the person anymore. Everyone believe they have the right to do anything. We live in a self-made world (my Interpretation of the world) where mankind want to be like God and they have forgotten what happened to the fallen creature that wanted the same thing **(Luke10:18)** and was kicked out of heaven. **(Then war broke out in heaven. Michael and his angels fought against the dragon, and the dragon and his angels fought back. But he was not strong enough, and they lost their place in heaven. The great dragon was hurled down—that ancient serpent called the devil, or Satan, who leads the whole world astray. He was hurled to the earth, and his angels with him Revelation12:7-9).** Mankind has adopted a new father who is a liar and the father of lies. The generation that behaved this way in the old days wanted to make a name for themselves and they brought division instead of unity **(Genesis11:1-10)** but thank God for Jesus who constantly intercedes for us before the Father. Our body is the temple of the Lord and we need to keep it holy for the coming back of Jesus. It is not enough to be born again, you have to walk in His principles and follow His instructions. You cannot pick what suits you or satisfy your feelings and leave the rest. God is love and everyone who loves Him must worship Him in spirit and in truth **(John4:24)**. The bible says if we speak in tongues, prophecy, have the knowledge of the bible and give all we have to the poor but do not love , it is nothing and we do not know God for God is love **(1Corinthians13:1-3; 1John 4:7-8)**. You cannot love God and love sin in the same vain for where God is, immorality cannot be present. God told Moses to take off his sandal because he was on a holy ground **(Exodus3:5)** and Joshua was told to take off his sandal by an angel **(Joshua5:15)** because he was standing on a holy ground.

⁋Unfortunately, those who follow Christ have compromised their belief to please the world and have adopted the world believes. The bible says we are in this world but not of the world. There is a reason why God told the people of Israel not to marry the foreign women and those who did adopted the gods the women worshipped and turned their hearts away from God (David, Solomon, Samson). Even Christian nations have consulted foreign gods instead of consulting God that was with their forefathers and who won battles for their fathers. **Why do the nations conspire and the peoples plot in vain? The kings of the earth rise up and the rulers band together against the Lord and against his anointed, saying, "Let us break their chains and throw off their shackles."" The One enthroned in heaven laughs; the Lord scoffs at them. He rebukes them in his anger and terrifies them in his wrath (Psalms2:1-4).** We live in a world where nations pass legislation that provokes heaven and angers God. Evil and wickedness are ruling the nations making it impossible for truth to prevail but do not be fooled, heaven and earth may fade away but none of His word will not go unfulfilled. What is happening in our world today does not come as a surprise to God- human beings search for love in awkward places when they should search for love from God who loves them unconditionally.⁋

The search for identity is sometimes the reason why people choose a life God has not called them to live. If you are confused about your identity it is because you are human. Everyone goes through a stage in their life when they are confused about their identity. During my teenage years, I went through an identity crisis. I did not know or appreciate who I was. Whatever suit me at that stage of my life that is what I called myself. At one stage, I was walking around with my chest pushed out because I wanted a bigger bust and a big bottom. That faze went away and then I decided at 11years of age to practice Islamic religion because I liked it and wanted to try other religions after all my dad was a non- practising muslim. Then at 15years old, my friends were having boyfriends and I wanted one but wanted someone who wanted to marry me. Who in their right mind would want to get married and have children at 15 years of age? My search for love that I did not get from my dad or mum made me to decide at an early age to settle down with any man who showed any interest in me. At that age I knew nothing about love apart from what I saw around me and on television. It is human nature to be confused but God is not confused. There was a son of a king (**Ammon**) who fell in love with his step sister. He was so obsessed with her that he made himself ill in order to sleep with the girl (**Tamar**). Immediately he got what he wanted he threw the sister out. A lustful desire and wrong advice from a shrewd friend killed him (**2Samuel13**). All sins start from somewhere and they are all the same, there is no small or big sin, sin is sin as Heaven is concerned. The bible says the wages of sin is death (**Romans6:23KJV**) but true repentance brings deliverance. Ammon had the right to have feelings if not he would not be human but what he did with the feelings is what brought him death. It is important to have a right role model at every stage of any identity crisis. Believers are not known to be doing a good job during these stages of life. It is either they are judgemental or compromise their belief. I recently read my journal dated 12/1/20. It was a message preached by Ray Bevan about how to guard ourselves from falling into dry places and refusing to fight the battle of life with emotional weapons i.e. feelings, wrong motives, selfish desires. As believers, the people we hang out with reflect the kind of people we are. You might disagree with that comment but I want to help you out. The fact that I speak to my neighbour who is gay does not make me gay but if I choose to hang out with him more than usual then my thoughts gradually begin to compromise what the bible says and before I know it I will soon be telling myself there is nothing wrong and even find a scripture in the bible that backs up my conviction. The bible says we are the light of the world. Our life should be what draws people to Jesus not the other way round. There is a saying that goes like this" show me your friend and I will tell you who you are". Who speaks to you? Who do you get advice from? Ammon chose a wrong person and it did cost him his life. Who do I give permission to speak into my life? Who controls my feelings and emotions? The world,society? What food do I give to my body, soul and spirit?

I noticed in the bible that every time people committed sexual immorality there was always repercussions on the land. When we choose to go against God's principles, we do not only suffer the consequences but generations after us also suffer. Great Britain as it is called took Christianity to various parts of the world but they failed to teach their children about God and now we have British born children who do not know anything about God except what it is taught in religious studies and you will even be lucky if the subject is taught by a true believer of Jesus Christ. I was once asked if I would sign a petition for homosexuality not to be taught in school. My response was if I know the content of what will be said I would not mind my child being taught as we live in a diverse world now and children need to know the things in a safe place especially from home. I went for training at work and the trainer was gay. There was a disagreement about whether to tell children about homosexuality at a younger age. But the way he explained the content the children would be taught, I was convinced it is the right thing to do but how awesome will it be if a believer will prayerful teach the children the heart of God on the subject? The bible says we should not be ignorant about what goes on around us. When we avoid talking about it in church, we push people to the world who will tell them things contrary to the word of God. The church of God must understand that God loves everyone but hates the sin people commit. Church has always been referred to as a hospital where people go to get well. When the Pharisees and the teacher of the law questioned Jesus for eating with the sinners Jesus replied, "It is not the healthy who need a doctor, but the sick. I have not come to call the righteous, but sinners to repentance." **(Luke5:31-32).**Our churches need to be equipped with good teaching to receive everyone. Unfortunately, many churches got it wrong and made people run to churches where homosexuals are welcome to practice what they believe. Christians are known to say one thing but do the opposite. We should be men and women of our words. If we say everyone is welcome it means we are able to respond to fears and confusion people may have. I am not saying the church should condone it but they need to create a safe platform where people can be free to speak out about their feelings and receive help to be delivered. SY Roger was bold to come out and tell his story. His voice did not change but his life changed because of mentors who believed in him and were willing to help him get the help he needed. Before his death in 2020, he was happily married with grown up children. Temptation is not a sin, even Jesus was tempted, and no one is beyond temptation. As seminars are run in churches to be successful in marriage and businesses, I believe there is a need for awareness and understanding about homosexuality in our churches. I do not expect you to agree with me on this but I know there is a need for spiritual insight into this. While we are preaching about prosperity and wealth and people are successful, morality is decreasing in the body of Christ. I really appreciate the boldness of Pastors who do not shy away to teach on right living in God. We will be liars if we say homosexuality is not in our congregation but what we do about it is what matters. Our Preachers must be bold and confident to rebuke in love and teach the true heart of God regarding the subject. I do not see the difference between abortion/ teenagers given condom/contraceptive pill and homosexuality. They are all wrong and it is up to you to believe what you want to believe. God or Man? Remember you cannot choose both. The bible says a friend with the world is an enemy with God **(Romans 8.7; James 4.4)**. You cannot serve two masters.

Be careful with emotions that make you to question or compromise your beliefs. Do you give in to your feelings every time i.e. talk like a woman/ dress like a woman/ behave like a man? Everyone is born differently, some people have a deep or soft voice, some grow beard and some do not. The fact that a woman has a beard and a deep voice does not make her a man. It is not unusual for a woman or man to speak a certain way. I mentioned earlier that the way individuals behave does not fit into one category. When we try to box things that is when it becomes complicated. All females cannot behave the same way neither can all males. We are unique to God who created us. The fact that someone wears tracksuits all the time does not make her a man. The fact that a boy likes to wear pink or purple does not make him a female. When my boys were growing up, I dressed them in pink and at some point they both loved red. Adults have a big role to play when it comes to this matter. If a child tells a parent that he thinks he is a girl because he behaves like one and that his school mates laugh at him because of the way he speaks, the parent needs to take this seriously and listen to the child and ask for God's wisdom on how to deal with the issue. The worst thing a parent can do is to rebuke the child, take the child to the pastor for a deliverance session. Obviously, if the parents cannot handle it they can take him to their pastor. This disclosure to me is not different to a child who says to his parent he has been abused. Many homosexuals get to adulthood before letting their parents know for the fear of rejection, rebuke or being disowned. Home is a safe place where children can express themselves. When my children told me what I can and cannot say outside, I used to let them understand that home is the only place I am free to be myself, no political correctness, no pretence, I don't have to apologise for my grammar. I must admit when my children were growing up, the way I handled the situations when they disclosed things to me was not the way I would handle them now that I am wiser and the holy spirit has taught me how to apply wisdom so that I do not push my children into the hands of the enemy who wants to destroy them. The holy spirt taught me and is still teaching me how to create a home that everyone is free to be who God wants them to be. A home where God is the centre of everything we do. We do not get everything right but we trust in the Father to help us.

I am grateful that God did not grant me some of my wishes during my identity crisis. I am glad God is not like human beings who make choices by how they feel because we would all be dead by now. As much as our feelings and emotions are good we cannot depend on them to lead us to do the right thing all the time. For example, a man finds himself falling in love with a married woman, even though he knows it is wrong, he is unable to resist this temptation. The bible says resist the devil and he will flee from you. Feelings feed on thoughts. What is in our thoughts? As a believer the bible always warn us about the state of our heart. **Finally, brothers and sisters, whatever is true, whatever is noble, whatever is right, whatever is pure, whatever is lovely, whatever is admirable if anything is excellent or praiseworthy think about such things. Whatever you have learned or received or heard from me, or seen in me put it**

into practice. And the God of peace will be with you (Philippians4:8-9). What do we watch/listen to? How much do we let what others say influences us? Who do we get counsel from? Who feeds our hearts? Words are powerful; once they come out they cannot be reversed. Our thoughts influence our words. What words are penetrating into our hearts? Lots of questions to think about before we agree or disagree on homosexuality. When we spend time with the people of the same sex, is it okay? It is not okay when we develop immoral feelings towards them? Two boys playing dad and mum roles does not make them gay. I was told that boys only schools might be the reason why some people choose this lifestyle. Whatever may be your reason it is wrong and God did not create a man to have a relationship with another man. I understand that young people like to experiment and are curious about the world they live in but I want to assure you that as a believer you do not need the world to tell you how to live a lifestyle that honours your Heavenly Father. When you gave your life to Christ old things passed away and now you are a new creature in Christ **(2Corinthians5:17)**. If you have found yourself thinking/ considering this lifestyle due to ignorance, now is the time to repent, ask God to forgive you and ask Him to help you to overcome this temptation. When you do that your sins will be forgiven and wiped away. **Therefore, God overlooked and disregarded the former ages of ignorance; but now He commands all people everywhere to repent [that is, to change their old way of thinking, to regret their past sins, and to seek God's purpose for their lives (Act17:30 AMP).**

We all have feelings and no one is perfect but we have the Holy Spirit of truth who will reveal the truth about the Father. The world can only fulfil the desire of the flesh not the spirit and as believers, we ought to live by the spirit not the flesh. I am single and I do have feelings too but I have to be self- controlled and let the Holy Spirit lead me not my flesh. Many times I have found myself attracted to wrong men but the Holy spirit helped me through the word of God and great friendships/ prayer partners showed me the heart of God for me. **And if Christ be in you, the body is dead because of sin; but t Spirit is life because of righteousness. But if the Spirit of him that raised up Jesus from the dead dwell in you, he that raised up Christ from the dead shall also quicken your mortal bodies by his Spirit that dwelleth in you. Therefore, brethren, we are debtors, not to the flesh, to live after the flesh. For if ye live after the flesh, ye shall die: but if ye through the Spirit do mortify the deeds of the body, ye shall live. For as many as are led by the Spirit of God, they are the sons of God. (Romans8:10-14KJV).** My understanding of what Paul was saying in this text is that the spirit must increase whilst my flesh die. I cannot feed my flesh every time it craves for lustful things. If you are diabetic, you cannot say because your body wants sweet things you should feed it, you will die before your time. Choose your feelings and make decisions that are right in the eyes of God. **But the fruit of the Spirit is love, joy, peace, forbearance, kindness, goodness, faithfulness, gentleness and self-control. Against such things there is no law. Those who belong to Christ Jesus have crucified**

the flesh with its passions and desires. Since we live by the Spirit, let us keep in step with the Spirit (Galatians5:22-25). For more reading, messages and books see recommendation.

PRAYER AND CONFESSION

I am grateful for the way God has created me I will not compromise my belief and sexuality. I will not twist the word of God to feed my feelings .I reject every evil advances

Zacchaeus was a chief tax collector and a wealthy man. He heard that Jesus was coming and he knew he would not be able to see Him because he was a short man. So he ran ahead and climbed the sycamore tree. But when Jesus got to where he was, He looked up and told Zacchaeus to come down and invited Himself to his house. Jesus ignored the people who were murmuring about Heating with a sinner and gave Zacchaeus and the rest of his household salvation **(Luke19:1-10).**

What is the short coming in my life? What attitude is in my life that wants to hinder my blessings? I place it before the Lord today.

Perseverance and persistent to know the truth about God will make room for me. What I thought is a disadvantage will turn to my advantage. I will not allow the enemy to use my weakness to condemn me of eternity. I will not listen to the lies of the enemy that I am a woman or I am attracted to men. I will not give permission to the world or let my feelings control my life rather I will give permission to the Holy Spirit to direct my thoughts, feelings, emotions and actions.

Nicodemus a Pharisee, teacher of the law and Jewish leader came to learn more from Jesus. He did not settle for only what the rabbi had taught him since he was a child. He wanted a new perspective and fresh understanding. Nothing is going to get in the way of inquiring for more knowledge. (**John3:1- 21).** My Ego, pride, arrogance, or fame will not stop me to seek for help in the area where I am struggling physically and spiritually. I will continue learning about God.

Blind Bartimaeus cried out to Jesus despite all odds against him. He was blind, he was told that Jesus was coming but when he tried to get Jesus's attention he was told to keep quiet but he shouted the more until the Lord heard him. When the Lord asked him what he wanted, he did not bit about the bush, he simply said "I want to see" and his eyes were opened. **(Mark 10:46-52).** How do people see me? How do I see myself? I am not what man calls me, I am who God called me. I was confused but now I can see clearly. I was blind but now I can see. I am not who I used to be, I am a new creation. I will not give up in the midst of the storm but persist until I receive my miracles. I will not be a victim of someone's misdiagnosis.

What is your Egypt? Egypt kept the people of Israel in bondage for many years but when the Lord turn their captivity they were like men who dreamt, their mouth was filled with laughter and their tongues with singing. Their enemies said 'The Lord has done great things for them' and we will also declare that 'The Lord has done great things for us and we shall be glad in the land' **(Psalms126:1-3).** I will be a man of integrity, honesty, honour and loyalty. A man who will not trade Godly principles to accommodate the works of the flesh.

I am an ambassador for Christ on earth, with whom many will come to know the Lord and accept Him as their Lord and saviour. A man that will not mislead people away from God. I will be salt and light for the world **(Matthew 5:13-16)**

Lust killed Shechem and all the males in his city **(Genesis 34).** Ammon was killed by his brother Absalom for defiling his sister **(2samuel13). Mark9:47** says **and if your eye causes you to sin, pluck it out, it is better for you to enter the kingdom of God with one eye than with two eyes and be thrown into the fire of hell.** I will not make choices that will bring shame or death. I will not lust after another man and I will not lust after things that will destroy my life and destiny. I will recognise lust and confess it to the Lord who will help me to overcome this desire. Above all, my action and decisions will not bring dishonour to my Father.

CELIBATE

The dictionary meaning of celibate is a person who abstains from marriage and sexual relations. **Now for the matters you wrote about: "It is good for a man not to have sexual relations with a woman." But since sexual immorality is occurring, each man should have sexual relations with his own wife, and each woman with her own husband (1Corinthians7:1-2).** A person who chooses not to have sex before getting married is not unheard of. It might be considered an ancient thing and it might not be popular in our days but it is possible. A man's first and foremost priority is to be faithful to his maker. No judgement on those who have had sex before marriage due to wrong teaching or past mistakes. The first man in the beginning was created first and from him came the woman. Each was created separately but for a purpose; to worship and honour the one who created them. Humanity kept changing the rules to suit them just like their fore fathers did in the Garden of Eden and brought judgement to themselves. Paul and Isaac were celibate until they got married.

In the 21st century, we are so quick to tell a boy what he should be or do but fail to educate him that sex is for when he is ready to be responsible and able to look after someone else. We are so quick to talk about sex education but fail to teach boys about girls and how to wait for the right moment. At the age of 6years old, some boys have already formulated (in their mind) what girls are like, based on their environment or what they have watched. Girls are not toys/barbies, or an experiment. At this age boys need help to go to school, attend to their personal hygiene and listen to bedtime stories. It is a shame that children carry these into adulthood and it has resulted into breakdown of marriages and homes. It is the responsibility of the adults to train up the children in the way to go so that when they are old they will not depart from it **(Proverb 22:6).**

Rejection is one of the big issues that men face and find difficult to get over. If this is not handled properly, it can cause suicide, murder, rape, bullying and abuse. I watched a TV series recently where a boy always got away with whatever he did. He killed his dog because the dog chewed his favourite ball and his parents did nothing about his behaviour. As he got older, his arrogance escalated into killing in public if things didn't go his way. He became so obsessed with a girl and he killed her brother. To cut the story short he ended up with a death sentence. When his parents visited him in prison, he asked them why they allowed him to do all the things he did and they did nothing? It was an emotional time for the parents but it was too late for him and even for them as there was no one to inherit all they had worked for. Celibacy is a choice and should be taught in schools and at home. Men should not be excluded from being celibate. As a man desires to marry a virgin, so should he also remain as a virgin for the woman he desires to marry. **Genesis 2:25 says Adam and his wife were both naked, and the felt no shame. There is no shame in being a celibate.**

Celibacy could be a waiting period. This is a moment where you are learning, observing, growing, imagining, experimenting, making mistakes and learning from them, making decisions and choices. This is one of the toughest decisions you have to make in your entire life. Society does not encourage it, families do not talk about it and schools fail to teach on the subject. Men need to know that it is okay to be alone; you are not weird if you do not have a girlfriend and you are not only created for sex. It is wrong to teach that a man needs a woman to be complete. He is made complete already, a suitable helper is what a woman is to him to share his goals and vision with. Celibacy is a decision, not everyone's cup of tea but for those who choose the path, let everyone around them support, embrace and appreciate them. **Now to the unmarried and the widows I say: It is good for them to stay unmarried, as I do. But if they cannot control themselves, they should marry, for it is better to marry than to burn with <u>passion.</u> (1 Corinthians7:8-9).**

What is your passion? It is possible that not every man will marry or become a husband. However, whatever you desire to be, make sure it is honourable to the Lord. I say this because I have seen uncles, brothers, sons, nephews who are as good as being alone than being married or having a family. In other words, be the man that God has created you to be. To know what God has created you to be ,spend time in His presence. That is why it is important to be taught this at an early stage of life to allow time to process the information and make your own decisions before life starts making decisions for you.

Be content and confident in who you are. Do not rush to get married when you are not ready and do not give in to peer pressure. Take the time to be who you desire to be in someone else's life. Celebrate being single and enjoy the helpers in your life. These can be your mother, niece, sister, aunt, grandma, foster mum, adopted mum, female neighbour/ employer/ employee. **For in Scripture it says: "See, I lay a stone in Zion, a chosen and precious cornerstone, and the one who trusts in him will never be put to shame." Now to you who believe, this stone is precious. But to those who do not believe, "The stone the builders rejected has become the cornerstone," and, "A stone that causes people to stumble and a rock that makes them fall." They stumble because they disobey the message— which is also what they were destined for. But you are a chosen people, a royal priesthood, a holy nation, God's special possession, that you may declare the praises of him who called you out of darkness into his wonderful light. (1 Peter2:6-9)** Be mindful and treat people around you the way you want others to treat you. That person in your life right now might be a link to the woman you have been waiting for or destined to marry. Many have missed the woman for their life because of their narrow mind about others. From an early age, I taught my children how to appreciate girls, so I was not surprised when one of my son's course mates at university complimented on the way he related with the ladies around him. My sons express their love for me in different ways. While some of our love languages are similar (of course, they came from me), some are unique to the individual. At a young age, I made my birthdays and other celebrations a big thing in our family (even though I am not a big fan) but I wanted them to understand that even though they do not love flowers, it does not mean that a friend doesn't and they should recognise it. I taught them to pay attention to the needs around them. At one point, I was so surprised when my son went to Body shop to buy something for a friend's birthday.

If you have made a decision to be a celibate, read about others who have gone ahead of you. What were their obstacles and how they overcame them so that you do not make the same mistakes? Many choose celibacy for different reasons. Whatever reason made you choose this lifestyle must be your go to every time you feel like quitting. For instance, if you are doing it for your faith, stick to it because if you mess it up it will be a disgrace to the faith and God. If you feel like you cannot carry on as a celibate then go ahead and get married. It is better to do the right thing than to burn with lust and to sleep around. **I wish that all of you were as I am. But each of you has your own gift from God; one has this gift, another has that. Now to the unmarried and the widows I say: It is good for them to stay unmarried, as I do. But if they cannot control themselves, they should marry, for it is better to marry than to burn with passion (1Corinthians7:7-9).**I believe celibacy is to set our self apart for God. Recognising that our body is the temple of God and making sure that our body glorifies God. Even if you have lived an immoral life before you came to the Lord, now that you are in Christ you are a new creature. The bible says; **if my people, who are called by my name, will humble themselves and**

pray and seek my face and turn from their wicked ways, then I will hear from heaven, and I will forgive their sin and will heal their land (2 Chronicles7:14)

By reading the bible, I learnt that our ability to do something is because the Lord has enabled us. No test or temptation that comes your way is beyond the course of what others have had to face. All you need to remember is that God will never let you down; he'll never let you be pushed past your limit; he'll always be there to help you come through it **(1Corinthians10:13).** We will not all be celibate for life but if you are graced to be, know that it is a gift and the gift is to honour God and help others in the body of Christ. Celibacy should not be kept to yourself, aim to educate the younger generation. It is okay to be private about this but it is also important to be bold and confident to talk publicly, creating a platform whereby young people know that it is alright to keep their body pure. Everybody has a story to share and your story might be the one that will keep a boy safe from a promiscuous life. At the age of 16years of age, I met two Christian brothers who really helped me to understand that I can stay single and pure for God at the time I had just rededicated my life back to God. I do not know what I would have done if they had not showed up the time they did. So, your testimony can save someone from making the biggest mistake of their life. Let people know why you have chosen this lifestyle, express your weakness and strength in the process. Thanks to celebrities who have come out openly about their season of celibacy i.e. Tim Tebow, Jordin Sparks, Kirk Cameron, Sean Lowe, Tamera

Mowry-Housley and many more. Having said this, during my research, I read about celebrities indulging in pornography to quench their desire for women /sex which is not right in the sight of God.

Celibacy is not something to be ashamed or guilty of, rather it should be embraced and celebrated. It might take awareness and education to get the older generation to understand this. You should not get tired or frustrated if you find yourself explaining over and over to grandad or grandma or even your parents that you do not want to marry someone just yet. Do not allow people to put unnecessary pressure on you. Celibacy is not an issue or a problem to get rid of in prayer rather it is a lifestyle to draw us closer to our first love. To the family or friend of someone who choose to be a celibate, it is important to listen attentively and allow the person to explain to you why they have made their decision. You need to realise that he has put a lot of thought into this and it has taken great courage to confide in you. Do not judge or discourage rather be careful when you are dishing advice and your opinion. Educate yourself about the subject, pray about it and let the Lord give you words to say to encourage him.

Parents; it is not what you have done or your parents have done that has made your son to decide to be a celibate. I do understand that you want to have grandkids but I want you to know that the small boy that was in your belly that has now become a grown up man is not only created to make babies. Be supportive and pray for him. Avoid questions like - why can't you be like so and so? When are you going to bring a girl home? When will I see my grandkids? I have come across parents who have given their grown up children an ultimatum to get married or they will cut them off their inheritance or disown them. Where is this in the bible if I may ask these parents?

I want us to look at the story of Joseph not necessarily because Joseph was a celibate but because I know that his story might encourage you to hold on to the decision you have made or about to make. Joseph had a dream which he shared with his family. **(Genesis37-48)**.The journey of life might resemble that of Joseph in the bible. He was hated for his gift of dreams, sold to slavery by his brothers, taken to a foreign land, but favoured in the house of Portiphar (a glimmer of hope which was cut short by Portiphar's wife obsession). He was thrown in jail for an accusation that was not true (injustice). While in prison, Joseph did not give up serving others and maintaining a moral life. He did not focus on his circumstances but focussed on how he could make a difference. His character did not change even though the circumstances around him changed. He refrained from complaining or seeking justice but trusted that God will fight for him and vindicate him one day. His gift made room for him and he was invited to the palace where he became second in command to Pharoah. His gift that his brother was afraid of or Portiphar's wife wanted to destroy became that which brought nations deliverance from hunger. Recognise and appreciate the gift that God has given you and use it for His purpose. Your gift and talent will make room for you and elevate you into greatness. Think carefully who you share your God given dream with.

Share your dream with people who will embrace it and give you constructive criticism, people who will be happy for you, support you and are willing to help bring forth the vision, people that will bring clarity and understanding to the dream. Celibacy is a good and beautiful thing whether for life or while waiting to get married.

PRAYER AND CONFESSSION

I thank You for the grace to keep myself pure until I get marriage or perhaps until You come back the second time.

Create in me a pure heart O God, and renew a steadfast spirit within me. Do not cast me from your presence or take your holy spirit from me. Restore to me the Joy of your salvation and grant me a willing spirit, to sustain me **(Psalms51:10-12).**

Give me the strength to keep my body holy and acceptable to you.

Give me the boldness to be in right standing with You

In the time of weakness, let me not give up but press on to the end. Let me trust that You will strengthen and uphold me with your righteous right hand. Let me believe and apply your word into the situation. In the moment of weakness protect me from myself or people that want to distract me and squash my decision.

I reject every lie of the devil that my decision will not work or I will fail. I will be like a tree planted by streams of water, which yields its fruit in season and whose leaf does not wither—whatever I do will prosper **(Psalms1:3).**

Help me to stay away from those who do not celebrate my dream.

The Lord will use the very thing that my enemy is afraid of to bless me. What was meant for evil the Lord will turn to joy **(Romans8:28)**. My enemies think they have won but they should watch the space, I am about to hit a jackpot. Checkmate I won.

When there is a delay in what God has promised me, I will be patient and not obstruct or interfere into what God is doing in the process.

My dream will cause men and women to bow down to God. The stone rejected by men will become the chief cornerstone **(Psalms118:22)**.

Like Joseph I will not repay back the enemies with the wrong they have done to me. Give me the grace to embrace the mistakes of those who have wronged me without a cause and bless those who hate me for no reason. Let me rely on God to avenge for me.

I am chosen, royal priesthood, holy, God's own possession who will declare the goodness of Him who has called me out of darkness into His marvellous light. **(1peter2.9)**

The unknown make people edgy, uncomfortable, suspicious and unsettled. When I find myself in the unknown, may I remain calm and trust God that He who has promised is able to do exceedingly and abundantly more than I can ask or imagine according to the power that works in me **(Ephesians3:20)**.

Reuben dishonoured his father by sleeping with his mistress and it cost him his birth right as the first son and his inheritance was given to someone who honoured their father. **(1 Chronicles5:1-2)**. O Lord of host, I will not dishonour my mum. I will not dishonour my dad. I will not dishonour the Lord.

COURTSHIP/DATING

Courting / dating time is exciting and enjoyable. But before you go into this season, I want you to ask yourself the following questions: Who is this girl? What is she bringing to my life? Who does she hang out with? What is her passion? What are her interests and hobbies? What motivates her? What is her belief/faith? What are her dislikes, likes and phobias? What is her relationship with her parents? What kind of home does she come from? (This is not to judge her, it is purely for you to understand her better since both of you are coming from a different background or perhaps culture) What do you both have in common? (This is what you will fall back on when there is challenges in the future) and many more questions which I know you would have thought about yourself. These questions are just to make you think deeper and explore more things you might not have considered. You cannot let your emotions get in the way of making a huge decision like marriage. Do not make a decision based on lust, obsession, pleasure it does not always end well. Get married for life not for a certain period. **Dear friend, pay close attention to this, my wisdom; listen very closely to the way I see it. Then you'll acquire a taste for good sense; what I tell you will keep you out of trouble. The lips of a seductive woman are oh so sweet, her soft words are oh so smooth. But it won't be long before she's gravel in your mouth, a pain in your gut, a wound in your heart. She's dancing down the primrose path to Death; she's headed straight for Hell and taking you with her. She hasn't a clue**

about Real Life, about who she is or where she's going. (Proverbs5:1-6MSG),

The bible says; two **are better than one (Ecclesiastes4).**When you are satisfied with what you have seen, then you can propose to her. Again, this is not a 101 steps to marriage; it is about you and your fiancée. If I may share my observation about this stage, most girls have dreamt about the day they will get married since they were 3 years old, so it is kind of special. Some men will run a mile at this stage because of the costs that it involves. May I remind you that money is not what matters but the thought that you put into giving a girl her dream. Again, women are different. Do your homework! Be yourself and go for what you can handle. Do not try to impress her but try to be the best. Be generous and kind. Be content and offer what you can. Do not go beyond your means. Do not give an impression you cannot keep up with when you get into marriage. Let your fiancée see you for who you are not the pretend you. Honesty and integrity is a virtue. Know who you are before you embark on the journey of marriage. Be trustworthy and take care of your body, soul and spirit. Do not neglect one for the other or pay too much attention to one than the other. If you notice a pattern in your life that you do not like, seek help and get rid of it. Even if it resurfaced in marriage, you can deal with it together with your wife. The bible says, two are better than one **(Ecclesiastes4: 9-11)**. I do not agree when people say things like, he was not like that before marriage, something must have triggered the behaviour. As much as I will not dispute that, I also believe that behaviour does not start in a day.

Behaviour might be dormant for years without even the person realising it is there but there will be signs that are probably ignored. If you keep telling yourself or people around you, "this is who you are and they should deal with it" then you have not allowed yourself to mature. Maturity is required in marriage to be able to accommodate the other person including your children. Cultivate a habit to self- assess yourself from time to time. I do this monthly to check my progress in life i.e. what have I achieved, what went well, what did not go as planned, mistakes I made and what I have learnt. Allow friends into your life who will give you honest and constructive criticism in order for you to mature. The bible says there are times to drink milk and there are times we have to eat meat **(1 Corinthians 3:1-3; Hebrews5:12-14).** This is not to say that you have to forget your charisma, what makes you laugh, silly, vulnerable and nevertheless to say, what makes you act childish. You cannot be too serious all the time that even the children cannot have play time with you. **Dear friend, if you've gone into hock with your neighbour or locked yourself into a deal with a stranger, If you've impulsively promised the shirt off your back and now find yourself shivering out in the cold, Friend, don't waste a minute, get yourself out of that mess. You're in that man's clutches! Go, put on a long face; act desperate. Don't procrastinate there's no time to lose. Run like a deer from the hunter, fly like a bird from the trapper! (Pro 6:1-5 MSG)**

Love yourself and love people around you. Know what biblical love is. What is your love language and the love language of your fiancée? It will help you to understand and relate to the one you desire to marry. Take good care of yourself and the body God has given you. Your body is the temple of the most high. Do not misuse your body or neglect to take care of it, God delights in everything that pertains to you. You are not a machine and you are not for every woman, you are for a woman who will help, support and love you for you. Keep your body and mind holy and pure for your maker. You only have one body, do not take it for granted. **Never take love for granted. Do you know the saying, "Drink from your own rain barrel, draw water from your own spring-fed well"? It's true. Otherwise, you may one day come home and find your barrel empty and your well polluted. Your spring water is for you and only you, not to be passed around among strangers. Bless your fresh-flowing fountain! Enjoy the wife you married as a young man! Lovely as an angel, beautiful as a rose—don't ever quit taking delight in her body. Never take her love for granted! Why would you trade enduring intimacies for cheap thrills with a whore? For dalliance with a promiscuous stranger? Mark well that God doesn't miss a move you make; he's aware of every step you take. The shadow of your sin will overtake you; you'll find yourself stumbling all over yourself in the dark. Death is the reward of an undisciplined life; your foolish decisions trap you in a dead end. (Proverbs5:15-23MSG).**

From observations, men are more likely to do well in their career more than their marriage because it is what gives them fulfilment and identity. Let your identity be in the Lord. Work will come and go but your self-worth, confidence, self-realisation, self-esteem and life will still remain with you. Do not put yourself in a situation where life has no meaning outside work. Create fun and hobbies for yourself. A place of interest, place to express your frustrations, place of peace, a solace, your go to when you need to clear your head. Alcohol, drugs, cigarettes, sex will not take your pain away, the devil might deceive you that it is the solution but he can only give you temporary fix. What about long term consequence these actions will create i.e. cancer, mental health issues, HIV, AIDS? Divorce is on the increase because of unfaithfulness and being in the wrong place at the wrong time. **So, my friend, listen closely; don't treat my words casually. Keep your distance from such a woman; absolutely stay out of her neighbourhood. You don't want to squander your wonderful life, to waste your precious life among the hard hearted. Why should you allow strangers to take advantage of you? Why be exploited by those who care nothing for you? You don't want to end your life full of regrets, nothing but sin and bones, Saying, "Oh, why didn't I do what they told me? Why did I reject a disciplined life? Why didn't I listen to my mentors, or take my teachers seriously? My life is ruined! I haven't one blessed thing to show for my life!"(Proverbs5:7-14MSG).**

By this stage of your relationship you should have an idea as to what your fiancée likes. Do not stay in a courtship in the name of she loves me or I love her when you are clearly not happy. YOU ARE NOT MARRIED. YOU CAN BE HAPPY WITH SOMEONE ELSE. Do not accept or condone abuse for the sake of love. For those crossing culture, it is essential you know and understand the culture. Be close to the family. Learn few things about the culture. Why? To make sure this is what you want and also to prepare yourself from any unpleasant comment/remarks from friends and family. Opinions from the public will not matter that much but it hurts when it comes from those who are close to you. Talk about this in detail. Look at scenarios that may or may not surface in the future. Read books to avoid any awkwardness and the feeling of rejection or not wanted. This is the best time to get to know your fiancée better. Not that you will know everything about her but it will give you a rough idea on the kind of woman you want to spend the rest of your life with. It is a mistake to assume that your fiancee will change or you will change them when you get married. That is why it is important to abstain from sex while courting so that if you feel the girl is not for you, you can call it quit and end the relationship without any hurt feelings.

I love her and she loves me is not enough. You need as much information as you can get before you step into courtship. When I was asked what the purpose of courtship /dating is, I decided to add this chapter as my response. Spend it wisely. The reason I wrote this chapter is for young people to understand what they can and can't do during this time. Again, I am not an expert, it is my own experience plus my understanding. There are so many Christian books on the subject; I will advise you to invest in some to enhance your understanding about marriage. (There will be some recommendation of the books that I have read at the end of the book).

WHAT SHOULD THE LENGTH OF COURTSHIP BE?

It is up to you on how long you want to stay in courtship for. I will strongly recommend your local church courses or counselling sessions, as knowledge is not too much and moreover the more you learn the more you understand your fiancée. Obviously, 'too much of anything is good for nothing' right! Stick to good counsel/ teaching / training.

What must you not do during courtship/dating? DO NOT LEAVE A GIRL HANGING/PLAYING GAMES: do not leave a girl hanging by showing her that you are interested in her when you are interested in someone else. Do not tell two ladies you love them at the same time (double date).This is not the way of the Lord and if you do not realise, you are hurting people and God will not be pleased with you for hurting His daughters. Do not constantly hang around a lady whereby everyone thinks you are dating but you are not and you ignore to correct the assumptions. Do not start a relationship with someone when you have no intentions of marrying them. Do not date a woman but have an eye for another. All this is cruel and evil. Pray earnestly about the girl you want to marry before you venture out. After having too many girls for too long you become a casanova and your self- worth is diminished and image tarnished. **Good friend, follow your father's good advice; don't wander off from your mother's teachings. Wrap yourself in them from head to foot; wear them like a scarf around your neck. Wherever you walk, they'll guide you; whenever you rest, they'll guard you; when you wake up, they'll tell you what's next. For sound advice is a beacon, good teaching is a light, moral** discipline is a life path. They'll protect you from wanton women, from the seductive talk of some temptress. Don't lustfully fantasize on her beauty, nor be taken in by her bedroom eyes. You can buy an hour with a whore for a loaf of bread, but a wanton woman may well eat you alive. Can you build a fire in your lap and not burn your pants? Can you walk barefoot on hot coals and not get blisters? It's the same when you have sex with your neighbor's wife: Touch her and you'll pay for it. No excuses. Hunger is no excuse for a thief to steal; When he's caught he has to pay it back, even if he has to put his whole house in hock. Adultery is a brainless act, soul-destroying, self-destructive; Expect a bloody nose, a black eye, and a reputation ruined for good. For jealousy detonates rage in a cheated husband; wild for revenge, he won't make allowances. Nothing you say or pay will make it all right; neither bribes nor reason will satisfy him. (Proverb 6 20-35MSG).

Courtship is not the time to double date or trying it out with a few women. It is the time to get to know your wife. At 29 years, Tamera Mowry-Housley revealed she only slept with her husband after marriage (Daily Mail By Chelsea White 19 July 2013). I like what she said in an interview with Ebony during the time of courtship: "Adam and I took a break from dating for about a year. We missed each other and something was drawing us together, but more than that, we wanted to make sure that this relationship was what God wanted for our lives. [In order to know] if we are meant to be together, we said, 'it's got to be God's way and not our way.' We didn't want to half-step anything [or have clouded judgment]. So our right way was the way we felt God wanted us to do it which was being celibate. We said to God, "This is who we are, I know you take us as we are, our faults, our fears, our joys, our hope as a couple and have your way." But if you want to be celibate, definitely don't live together [laughs] because that makes it harder for you. Have people around you to keep you accountable! Surround yourself with people who support your decision because they're only going to root for you. Make that covenant with God and with each other and just let go. God is going to see you through the difficult times. Whenever you're feeling discouraged, pray together. Like I said it's not going to be a perfect journey, but you just have to keep God at the centre of your relationship (Tia and Tamera on Marriage and Motherhood By Brookes Obie October17, 2012). Perhaps, you have slept together and you are wondering if you will have a good marriage. Repent, ask God to forgive you and refrain from sleeping together until you get married. Purify yourself, what we do after sinning is what matters to God.

A man or woman will not have an answer to everything. In fact you will get things wrong , make mistakes and fail in some areas but if you are faithful and diligent your time spent in courtship will lead to a long lasting marriage. **The bible tells us to seek God first and all other things will be added to us (Matthew 6:33). Be accountable to do what it right in the eyes of God. You are not perfect, God is. Do not try to figure everything out in your own strength. Trust in the Lord with all your heart and lean not on your own understanding; in all your**

ways submit to him, and he will make your paths straight. Do not be wise in your own eyes; fear the Lord and shun evil. This will bring health to your body and nourishment to your bones (Proverbs3:5-8). If at any stage of your courtship you feel confused, it is a clue for you to take a step back and consult God for more insight as to why you are feeling the way you are. Do not ignore your feelings, God gave them to you for a reason. If you and your partner are struggling in a particular area, seek counsel (this is when those church sessions become handy). Make sure both of you are in agreement not one sided relationship where one talks too much and the other keeps quiet because she/he was not given a chance to express their opinion. Enjoy your courtship. I always say your courtship is a preview of how your marriage will be. What you do and how you do things determines what kind of marriage you will have. Do things according to biblical principles. I like that Tamera and her husband decided at the beginning of their courtship to do things God's way not their way. When we put God first and at the center of what we do, we have assurance that all will be well and when challenges come we can go back to God. The bible says: **Bring the whole tithe into the storehouse, that there may be food in my house. Test me in this," says the Lord Almighty, "and see if I will not throw open the floodgates of heaven and pour out so much blessing that there will not be room enough to store it (Malachi 3:10).** This test is not only in our tithes and offering but everything we do i.e. our sacrifice to follow His principles and teachings, our obedience to do the right thing and honour God with our body, our commitment to show the world the true meaning of love and marriage and above all demonstrate God's love to humanity. (No pressure but our marriage is a mirror of a marriage between heaven and earth and the relationship between God and man).

PRAYER/CONFESSION

Thank God for the grace to find the right woman for your life

Thank God for steering you in the right direction even when your mind is wandering off from the girl God has for you

Thank God for this season of courtship and dating

I commit this season of my life into your hands Lord. Direct and guide me

Let me keep my body Holy during this time of courtship

Help me to focus on the girl God has given me and protect me from other girls who want to distract me

Open my eye to see areas that need to be change and let me be willing to change. Let me enjoy my courtship

Let me use this time wisely and not just be thinking about the flesh

Let me focus on God to help me to know and understand this lady

Let me be disciplined with my time, money and body

Give me self-control when I am around my fiancée. Let me not lust after unrighteousness. In the moment of weakness, give me strength and give me the ability to wait until the day of our wedding

Let me be faithful to my fiancée. I will not take love for granted.

If this lady is not my wife Father reveal it to me and let me hearken to Your voice. Let me pay close attention to what You are showing me in this season. I will pray at all time and follow Your instructions

A man of understanding will attain to wise counsel, I will not follow wrong advice and counsel

I will not walk in the counsel of the ungodly or sit in the seat of the scornful but my delight will be in the Lord and in His word I will meditate day and night **(Psalms1:1-2)**

The bible says whoever finds a wife finds a good thing and obtain favour from the Lord, this lady will bring goodness to me and I will be a good man to her. I release your blessing on our courtship **(Proverbs 18:22)**

I separate myself from seductive women. Ladies who want to lure me away from God's purpose for my life

I will not to defile my bride before marriage

I refuse to listen to people who want to bring conflict between me and the lady I intend to marry

God You do not bring confusion, when the journey of courtship/dating looks confusing, I ask for insight and wisdom. Shed light to every uncertain situation and bring clarity to cloudy situations.

When Jacob thought Esau will kill him, Esau ran to meet him, embraced and threw his arms around his neck and kissed him and they both wept. **(Genesis33:4).** What is your worry or concern today? The King of Kings is greater than the situation you are facing. I will not be consumed or overwhelmed by what is going on around me because I know God will meet me at the point of my needs. God's hand of grace is wrapped around me to sooth every broken issue in my life.

Jacob knew what he did to his brother before he left home, how he took his brother's blessing causing his brother to be angry and wanting to kill him. But on the day he met with his brother, he humbled himself **(Genesis33:5).** My father and my God, may I realise when I am wrong to humble myself, apologise and do what is right. Arrogance or pride will not rob me of my blessing.

Teach both of us to be humble, tolerant and be patient with each other

It is a blessing to find a virtuous woman but it takes grace to keep her. Father, I ask for grace to do what is right by this lady

Forgive the way I have treated ladies in the past. Show me your way.

EUGENE'S STORY

This chapter is dedicated to a very faithful husband and father - Eugene. I was so moved by Eugene's journey from single to married life that I decided to put it in a chapter. The interview was meant to be for 10-20 minutes but we ended up chatting for an hour. Even though I have known Eugene through Angela over the years, I was not sure what to expect and it broke the barrier I have had of not being able to have a conversation with men. I am grateful that Eugene made it easy for me and the conversation that seemed difficult for me was made possible. I am grateful for his honesty and above all thanks to Angela who agreed for me to interview her husband. I can clearly see how their marriage works so well. I pray that God will continue to bless their marriage and home. I learnt so much from this conversation and what I have written in marriage, husband and father finally made sense. I trust God that you will be blessed. Below is the interview I had with Eugene (Q=question asked by Tola and R=response given by Eugene)

Q- When did you give your life to Christ? R- I do not know for certain when I came to know the Lord because Christ like behaviour, doing good and church has always been with me growing up. My parents made sure that the principles, practices, training and foundation at home were God centred. After university, I did not practice Christianity or mature in Christ. I followed the crowd, drew away from God and chasing after money and position became my priority. Even though I tried to do good at this stage of my life, reading my bible and maturing in Christ was not what I practiced.

Q- What is the journey now that you have reconnected with God? R- It has changed for the better but not completely changed. There are still some bad habits that need to improve but I am acknowledging what Jesus would do in a situation and recognising the Holy Spirit and the power of healing. It is a struggle to be a better Christian because the mind is a battlefield, you just have to be positive, drag yourself from old ways and be more conscious of your actions and behaviour

Q- What are the struggles as a believer? R- Unforgiveness when someone hurts me. I do not forgive the person or let go or forget what the person did .Even when I try to forget sometimes the hurt comes back and I bring it up every time they say/do something, it is like a shadow. I am conscious and praying about this because I believe healing is a process. I want to be 'intentional' about forgiveness

Q- How would you describe yourself? R- Conscientious, I think about people and am mindful of others.

Q- How did you meet your wife? R- At work. She was going to Seven sisters to look for work but found herself in Seven kings and was directed to where I worked in White chapel.

Q- How did you know she was the one for you? R- We got along and my brother told me I would marry her. We courted for 5 years then got married

Q - What attracted you to Angela? R- Her perspective is totally different from mine and other girls I had dated. I had this Nigerian mentality of what I knew about women and what my father told me about not to marry a white woman. What I saw in Angela was totally and completely different from my thinking.

Q- How is married life? R- Exciting and at the same time we are still getting to know each other. We enjoyed the company of each other for 5 years until the children came. The only thing I regret is not listening to Angela to do some travelling because of my Nigerian mentality of working, saving and not waste money.

Q- What is your relationship with the children? R - Brilliant but there are things I still have to work on. I get on well with them but I have this weakness that if I give them what they want (i.e. money, roof over their head, good education) then that is enough but I have realised now that our relationship matters. I need to get to know them and their world. I try to get involved in their life but I think because I did not have that kind of relationship with my parents and I came out okay, the boys will be fine. I need to listen more to the children, start picking clues and be quick to respond. I and Angela work together and complement each other. Where Angela is weak, I am strong, where Angela is strong, I am weak.

Q- What stops you from having an intimate relationship with the boys? R- My Nigerian background and myself. Not knowing or recognising a problem but once I know I jump to it straightaway, make corrections and change. I hated confrontation. If

I notice something, I will ignore it, not confront it or shy away from it until it hits me in the face. I allow things to linger and wait days before solving situations. I want peace way too much.

Q- Why do you think you act/ think this way? R- At work, I am able to put people in their place but when it comes to my home, I feel I do not want to rise to the challenge of correcting them whereby hurting them.

When asked how his relationship with his wife reflect on the children? He said there is a collaboration, partnership and agreement between them. A good role model for the children.

Q- How does your parents' marriage make you a better father and husband? R - My Dad believed in being equal with my Mum in terms of help around the house. He totally supported my mum at home. For example; my Dad would never wake my Mum to clean and I have incorporated that in my home. This has made me appreciate my Dad even more. My Mum's love of church, God and Christianity had a massive impact in my life. Around finances and money, my Dad was my inspiration. When my Mum passed away, Dad had to take care of the house responsibilities and when he lost his job, he had to step up, apportion money for different needs in the house.

Q- What did you see in your parents that you chose not to repeat in your marriage? R- In times of trouble or arguments do not do it in front of the children but do it behind closed doors. Angela and I deal with issues when the children are not around but at the same time we let them know that we are two different people with different personalities and we are bound to make mistakes or disagree.

Q- What advice will you give young people? R- Learn to walk in love with other people around you. Everyone has a God given temperament and come from different backgrounds. Understand people's strength, weaknesses and personalities for it will help you live at peace with others. We cannot be the same, young people need to understand that people are different from them and allow people to be who they are. This principle will help them to mature quicker.

Q- What advice will you give a man struggling with life/ marriage? R- Acknowledge and realise that you cannot do it by your own understanding or strength. You must put God first and in the centre. Let the Lord's hand be on all you do. Have faith in God. Then, know your strength, know that today will never be like tomorrow. You can improve things by bringing the positive side of you out and be who you are. For those struggling in marriage, take a step back; write good things about your wife and the negatives. If you look at it you will find out that there is more positive than negative. In crisis we tend to see more negatives than positives but when you take a step back to reflect you will see something different. Work with the negatives; give her time to change and move towards the positives.

Q - How do you manage friendships outside the home? Do you still maintain friendship with people you knew before you got married? R- I kept some of my friends from before I got married and I make new friends as well as long as they align with the principles of marriage. I made up my mind that I can be friends with someone who is not married but I shouldn't let them affect me. You do not want to be friends with someone that will poison your mind against your wife or home.

PRAYERS AND CONFESSIONS

The way I train my child/children will be a light for many to follow. My parenting skills will cause others to want to have children.

As my children grow older they will not turn out like **Achan** who coveted the plunder of Babylon and brought death to himself and his entire household **(Joshua7)** or **Doeg** an antagonist of David who caused the death of a large number of priests **(1Samuel21:7 & 22:9-23)** or **Abishai** who used his authority to kill innocent people because of hate and un –forgiveness **(1 Chronicles18:12-13, 1Samuel 26:9).** But my children will be like **Boaz** who looked after a widow/stranger and did not take advantage of her, a warrior like Gideon **(Ruth 2-4).** A worshipper like **David** who is not afraid to stand up to anyone who defiles God **(1Samuel17).** A dreamer like **Joseph** who delivered a nation from poverty during the season of famine, a foreigner that became a Prime Minister **(Genesis37; 39-41). Daniel,** a foreigner in Babylon who was promoted to become a governor **(Daniel2).**

Lord, give my child/ children dew of heaven, plenty of grains, fatness of the earth and a new wine **(Genesis27: 28-29).** He /she will sing a new song and be given opportunities, favour, projects, job everywhere he/she goes. Nations will bow and serve my child/ children like Jonathan who saved a friend from death (**1 Samuel 19**)

When my child comes to me for counsel, may I discern to give right counsel. Holy Spirit teach me what to say, let my motives be pure, show me his/her motives behind what he/she is asking me. May I not be consumed with my thoughts that I miss or ignore the important information about my child. My counsel will not be based on material or worldly things but influenced by the Spirit of God. May my heart be pure towards my child **(Psalms 51: 6-8)**

Isaac sent Jacob to Rebekah's family to marry. Open my eyes to see the wife or the family my sons will marry, so that when they present her to me, my judgement and emotions will not be compromised by what I see**(Genesis28)**. Eli turned a blind eye to the atrocity his children caused in the land and refused to reprimand them. David refused to do something about his children's behaviour. Father, help me to pay attention to my children's behaviour as you pay attention to me. May I never avoid condoning sin, allowing my children to run riot and do nothing. I will not ignore bad behaviour but I will correct with love. I will not be afraid to discipline my children when they disobey me. For the child you love you discipline **(Proverbs 3:12)**. Give me wisdom to detect what is a lie and what is truth. May I discipline my child according to God's command. May I not lose heart and grow weary to discipline them **(Hebrews 12:3)**.

Daddy, bless my union with love, harmony and praise. Join us with the cord that cannot be broken. Let my matrimonial home be peaceful. A home I can find solace and rest, a home I long to go to after a long day at work. Father, You will be the ultimate in my home. We will not wander away from Your counsel, precept and Your instruction.

When there is a misunderstanding or conflict between me and my wife, the Lord will give us insight and wisdom on how to resolve it. We will not allow un-forgiveness to rule in our home. We ask for patience to listen to one another. Be quick to listen, slow to speak and slow to be angry **(James 1:19)**.In everything, we will give thanks to God and honour His name. In sickness and in health we will celebrate each other. In lack and plenty we will appreciate each other. What brought us together will be the key to keep us together for the rest of our life. My thought towards my wife will be pure, true, noble, lovely, admirable and praise worthy **(Philippians4:8-9)**.

There is no justification in revenge, if my wife has done anything evil to me, I give my feelings to the Lord and let God carry the pain for me. The Lord knows the best way to handle it. My emotion will not cause me to sin against God. Amen

MARRIAGE

This chapter is designed for those who are planning to get married and those already in marriage. Marriage is ordained by God **(Genesis 1&2)** and it is between a man and a woman who come together in a holy matrimony, to commit to each other until death. **Then the Lord God made a woman from the rib He had taken out of the man, and he brought her to the man. The man said, "This is now bone of my bones and flesh of my flesh; she shall be called 'woman,' for she was taken out of man." That is why a man leaves his father and mother and is united to his wife, and they become one flesh (Genesis2:21-24).** Who is this bone of your bone and the flesh of your flesh? Look at yourself in the mirror. What do you see? Think about the following questions properly, to help you to figure out who you are if you haven't already: Am I patient, am I kind? Do I envy, do I boast, am I proud, do I honour others, am I self-seeking? Am I easily angered, do I keep a record of wrongs, do I delight in evil or I rejoice with the truth? Do I always protect, trust, hope and always persevere? If you can honestly answer the above then you will know who the bone of your bone and flesh of your flesh is or should be.

When you were a child, you talked like a child; you thought like a child and reasoned like a child. When you became a man, you put the ways of childhood behind you **(Corinthians 13:11)**. Marriage is for men not for children. I do not mean this in a disrespectful way but it is true. You can teach a child to swim but you cannot make that child to swim. Marriage is for two people who have made a commitment to each other to stay together for better or for worse. So the man gave names to all the livestock, the birds in the sky and all the wild animals. But for Adam no suitable helper was found, **(Genesis 2:20).** Who is this helper? What does she look like? Where would I find her? There is a saying where I come from, that whatever you are looking for in a town called Sokoto, is in the trouser called Sokoto. In other words what you are looking for might be closer than you think. Quit looking at the outward appearance, look inward. I must say that marriages that last do so by the grace of God, it is not because they are better than those who did not make it. Your bone and flesh is from you. Eve was taken from the ribs of Adam, suggesting that your wife to be must complement you. Where do you think your suitable helper is going to come from? These are some of the questions you might need to consider first before you start the journey of marriage. One of the things I have observed from long and lasting marriages is that they work together not against each other. I used to suffer from lupus where your immune system works against every part of your body and I can tell you it is painful, depressing and draining. No matter how hard I used to fight to get better, when lupus triggered, it took me back to square one. It was like taking a step forward and ten steps backward. This is what marriage looks like when both parties do not work together.

Marriage is a partnership. In marriage there needs to be a compromise, perseverance, tolerance and endurance. The language spoken in your home should be about 'us' not about 'me'. Celebrate each other's talents and gifts, understand each other's strength and weaknesses. Work together. In marriage you do not close your eyes, you go in with your eyes wide open. Meaning you make a commitment to make it work i.e. when things go wrong in marriage, you deal with these things together. Do not make a decision based on anger or not understanding what the other person is talking about. What do you intend to get from this marriage instead of your fantasy about marriage? Can you give what it takes to stay in a marriage? Can you commit to this in a long run? The lifespan of a marriage does not depend on age or maturity, poor or rich but individual understanding and contributions towards it. Marriage is like purchasing a plant in the supermarket, as long as you keep watering and nurturing the plant it will keep growing and flourishing but if you neglect it, it will die. Marriage is not for everyone, but if you chose to get married, do it for the right reason and trust that the person you partner with is the bone of your bones, and flesh of your flesh.

As a believer, you cannot have sex outside marriage. In the 21st century, many have compromised the command of the Lord due to peer pressure, lust, pleasures or the norm. Please refer to the previous chapter about how to keep your body pure for the Lord. Husbands, keep your body pure for your wife. Be faithful and remain faithful throughout your marriage. **Now for the matters you wrote about: "It is good for a man not to have sexual relations with a woman." But since sexual immorality is occurring, each man should have sexual relations with his own wife, and each woman with her own husband. The husband should fulfil his marital**

duty to his wife, and likewise the wife to her husband. The wife does not have authority over her own body but yields it to her husband. In the same way, the husband does not have authority over his own body but yields it to his wife. Do not deprive each other except perhaps by mutual consent and for a time, so that you may devote yourselves to prayer. Then come together again so that Satan will not tempt you because of your lack of self-control. I say this as a concession, not as a command. I wish that all of you were as I am. But each of you has your own gift from God; one has this gift, another has that (1Corintians 7). There is no marriage that does not go through challenges. If there is a problem in your marriage at the moment, find out where it is coming from then face and resolve it together. Seek Godly and professional help to support you in the area you are struggling with or situations that keep interfering in your marriage. I will be cautious about friends counselling you as their judgement or advice might be compromised by what they already know about you.

It takes time, hard work, consistency, communication and being vulnerable with one another in order to build a home. Do not ignore a crisis, silence, bad mood, heavy drinking or smoking, compulsive spending or constant nagging. It might be a cry for attention or something. Deal with it before it escalates beyond your control. Do not give room for the devil to come in and steal, kill and destroy your marriage. If you have neglected your partner before or taken them for granted, today is the day to repent and apologise. Remember God loves your marriage and he will do anything to keep you together and send help to you if you are willing to change. Listen to His whisper, He is there to comfort, help, counsel, intercede, advocate, strengthen and stand by you in every season. Keep your eyes on the goal, that very thing that draw you together is the very thing that will keep your marriage. Do not lose the driver, the 3rd party in your marriage the bone of your bone, and the flesh of your flesh wants to be part of your success, pain and struggles. Let her in. She is not in your life to decrease, minus, subtract or divide but to increase, add-on and multiply you. She is your wife not a devil sent to destroy you. Her attitude or behaviour might look like she is your enemy but she is not, deal with that behaviour in prayer. The bible says resist the devil and he will flee from you. I have seen and witness some women behaving badly. Again I am not to judge as I am not sure what triggered the behaviour because I was not there. This is why you need to know your wife so that when there is a change in behaviour you are the first to recognise it and find solution for it. Do not ignore bad behaviour or condone it, try and resolve it with your wife with love (of course). There are some ladies who are just difficult to please or understand but God will give you the grace and patience you need. Do not have the attitude to 'get out' at any slightest hurdle, stay and work it out with your wife. The bible says, you have to love your wife like Christ loves the church that he gave his only son to die for them **(Ephesians 5:25)**. Constantly commit to the Lord, the woman you are about to marry or the woman you are married to.

Finally and most importantly, invite God into your marriage. Do not lose sight of Him and if you have done so, get back on track. There is a story in the bible where Jesus went to a wedding and the wine was finished. Cutting the story short, after the Lord had turned the water into wine, the guest of honour told the bridegroom that normally everyone brings out the good wine first and then the cheaper wine after the guests have had too much to drink but this wedding had saved the best till the end (**John2**). After you have done all you can, leave the rest to the Lord. It is sad when you hear abuse, divorce, separation in Christian marriages. This is not God's intention when he instituted marriage. In my opinion, separation or divorce happens either because the marriage started on a wrong foundation or whatever has happened was neglected or the couple took their eyes off the ball. Be attentive to the details of your marriage. Refuse to allow outsiders to tell you what you should know about your marriage.

It is her fault will not get you anywhere. We clearly see this in the beginning of creation, where God asked Adam why he ate the fruit He commanded him not to eat and the only logical answer Adam could come up with was that 'the woman you gave me gave me the fruit and I ate it' (**Genesis3:12**). Admit when you are wrong and ask how you can make things better. Even when you are not wrong, apologise anyway. A man once told me the secret of his lasting marriage is to apologise for everything even when it is not his fault and that kept peace in their home. You are not perfect and that is why God created a suitable helper for you. Do not exchange marriage for fame or career or money or another woman. I heard a story about a man who was always working and spent little time with his wife and children. Everyone at work liked him, he was always doing something for everyone. He built a big house in his home country but died from covid19. His pension and hard-work was enjoyed by someone else as he lay in bed lifeless and no one could help him. His colleague, friends, people he spent most of his time with could not take this horrible nightmare from him. He died just like that, back to dust, vanity upon vanity. Cherish what you have and what you do not have. Enjoy every moment and make every moment count. Laugh even in your arguments, mistakes and failures. Marriage is not a show to the world; it is about who you are and who you become through the Holy Spirit.

A soft answer turns away wrath: but grievous words stir up anger. The tongue of the wise uses knowledge aright: but the mouth of fools pours out foolishness. The eyes of the Lord are in every place, beholding the evil and the good (Proverb15:1-3) Do not go to sleep with unresolved issues. Even though your wife does not want to talk about it, that does not excuse you from talking about it. Talk to your father about it. Let Him give you guidance and direction on how to resolve the issues. Refuse to create a place in your marriage for an intruder. **The thief does not come except to steal, and to kill, and to destroy. I have come that they may have life, and that they may have it more abundantly (John10:10).** The thief is roaming about looking for marriages to devour, let it not be yours. His main aim is to steal, kill and destroy your marriage. Your wife is not the devil, she is not your enemy but your companion. She not your punching bag/ slave either but your helpmate who will eventually become the mother of your children. She is definitely not your mother and she is not your past but your present. **Therefore humble yourselves under the mighty hand of God, that He may exalt you in due time, casting all your care upon Him, for He cares for you. 8 Be sober, be vigilant; because your adversary the devil walks about like a roaring lion, seeking whom he may devour. Resist him, steadfast in the faith, knowing that the same sufferings are experienced by your brotherhood in the world (1peter5:6-9 NKJV).**

I do not have a magic wand or answers to all your questions or what you are going through in your marriage but if you diligently and carefully obey God's instructions and follow them, you will enjoy your marriage. I am not saying you will not go through hard times because you are a believer but His grace will be sufficient for you. I have seen evidence of God's faithfulness in marriages. I have seen broken marriages being restored. God is the one that can mend the broken heart, forgive and allow God to heal your pain. Just as a wound takes time to heal, forgiveness is a process, it will take time, willingness and patience. Give yourself time to heal and your marriage a chance. **"Now Abraham was old, [well] advanced in age; and the Lord had blessed Abraham in all things. Abraham said to his servant [Eliezer of Damascus], the oldest of his household, who had charge over all that Abraham owned, "Please, put your hand under my thigh [as is customary for affirming a solemn oath],and I will make you swear by the Lord, the God of heaven** and the God of earth, that you will not take a wife for my son from the daughters of the Canaanites, among whom I live, but you will [instead] go to my [former] country (Mesopotamia) and to my relatives, and take a wife for my son Isaac [the heir of the covenant promise]." The servant said to him, "Suppose the woman will not be willing to follow me back to this country; should I take your son back to the country from which you came?" Abraham said to him, "See to it that you do not take my son backthere! The Lord, the God of heaven, who took me from my father's house, from the land of my family and my birth, who spoke to me and swore to me, saying, 'To your descendants I will give this land'—He will send His angel before you [to guide you], and you will take a wife from there for my son [and bring her here]. If the woman is not willing to follow you [to this land], then you will be free from this my oath and blameless; only you must never take my son back there." (Genesis24:1-8AMP)

This text is not saying you should arrange a wife for your son. The Canaanites are like unbelievers if you like and they worship idols and many times in the bible the Lord always warned the people of Israel not to marry foreign women who would lure them to worship other gods and cause them to sin. We saw this in Solomon. As much as he did great things for the Lord, his foreign wife turned his heart away from God causing him to do evil in the sight of God. What does this mean in the 21st century? Do not marry a woman who does not believe in the God that you believe. Do not compromise your faith in order to marry. Do not allow fame, wealth, riches, beauty blind you from making the right decision when choosing a woman to marry. What do I do to find a wife God intended for my life? Pray, spend time with God and let the Holy Spirit direct you. Charm is deceitful and beauty is vain, but a woman who fears the Lord, shall be praised **(Proverbs31:30AMP). But the Lord said to Samuel, "Do not consider his appearance or his height, for I have rejected him, The LORD does not look at the things people look at. People look at the outward appearance, but the Lord looks at the heart." (1 Samuel16:7).** Most men get stuck on how to express their love to their wife in the language she will appreciate/understand. Not all ladies love flowers or cards, find what arouses your wife. Give surprise gifts, take her out often. Notice her and let her know that you love and care about what she cares about. Show interest in what she loves. Sex is great but it is not the answer to everything. Find what both of you are passionate about. A good friend will tell his friend when he is going in a wrong direction. As you are your wife's friend, you should give constructive criticism with love. Remember, if she smells nice, people will praise you because she is part of you.

For words or poems to rekindle your marriage see songs of songs

PRAYER AND CONFESSIONS

I thank God for the bone of my bone and the flesh of my flesh. May I recognise her among thousands of women.

I ask for divine connection to meet the lady God has destined for me to marry. A woman that believes in the God that I believe.

Isaac was meditating when he saw Rebekah **(Genesis24:63),** I will live a lifestyle of meditating and inquiring from God. Let me see God's word as the answer to all my problems.

I will not choose a wife out of fear, peer pressure or pressure from parents or society.

I will not choose Delilah **(Judges 16),** a woman who will do anything to expose my secrets to the world. A woman that will connive with my enemy to harm me. A woman who will take away my glory and greatness. A woman that would keep me bound under her spell and humiliate me.

I reject a wife like Eve, whose desire to gain wisdom will cause me to disobey God and lose blessings deemed for me **(Genesis3:6).**

Deliver me from a promiscuous woman. **(Proverbs 5-7).**

A woman that is unstable in all her ways will not come my way. Remove from my path a woman that will distract me from the one God has destined for me. But bring my way a woman that operates in the gift of the spirit. A helper who will understand me and be my comfort when I am hurting. A woman willing to submit to my authority. The one who is humble and will support me **(Genesis 24:18).** The one who will gel with God's plan and purpose for my life, who will be a blessing not a curse. A woman that is content with what she has and not obsessed with what she does not have. A woman that will bring the best out of me. In return, I ask that I will be a man who honours and respects the woman and will not defile her until the day of our wedding. I will love her and shower her with gifts **(Genesis 24:22).** I will include the woman in my decision making. My ego and pride will not come between me and my wife.

I will make my woman happy and bring the best out of her. I am believing for a beautiful woman inside and outside. A woman that loves and honours her parents as God commanded and she is willing to accommodate my parents. Lord bring a good, devoted, lover of God family to choose a wife from, not deceivers/users like Laban **(Genesis29-31)**

I will ask the woman's parents for their permission to marry their daughter. I will be loved and accepted by my in-laws. May my in-laws deal kindly and truthfully with me. Her parents will pray and bless our relationship. (It is not too early or late to pray these prayers for your son if you are a parent or grandparent).

My wife and I will not invite a third party that will destroy our home (third parties can be gambling, excessive drinking, misuse of drugs, people, outlaws, lies or another woman).

I will multiply, be fruitful and flourish in child bearing. I will not be barren or childless. There will not be complication in child bearing. If it is my desire and an agreement between my wife and I not to have children, may God's blessing be upon us. May people around us understand and respect our decision. The pressure will not overwhelm us. When there is a delay in child bearing, give myself and my wife grace to wait patiently for Your timing. A child like Samuel is worth waiting for. Give us peace, joy, endurance and tolerance while waiting.

I will love my wife and be willing to do anything to support her just like Jacob rolled away the large stone for Rachel so that she could feed her flocks **(Genesis29:1-10).**

I refuse the spirit of laziness. I will understand the concept of working (sowing and reaping) and enjoying the labour of my sweat. I will work hard for my money rather than fast track into money I am not ready to handle. I will be content with what I have

I will be faithful to my wife. There will never be another woman. I will not marry or go out with a woman that is ungodly, seductive, wicked and cause me to sin like Solomon. I see a long time relationship and marriage. No room for separation and divorce. I cancel divorce and separation by the blood of Jesus. If I have allowed sin that led to separation, Father forgive me. Give me wisdom to bring us together. I do understand that I am not perfect and I will make mistakes. When I do, give me humility to own up to my mistake and ask for forgiveness. Help us to forgive each other when we make mistakes.

I understand that there are some secrets that will come out as we spend time to get to know each other more. Father, give me the grace to handle my wife's secrets. May we trust each other and give me maturity to look beyond my wife's flaws. Let us allow each other to work our journey of faith, weaknesses and past. May I be a source of support not a hindrance in the process of recovery from loss/illness.

I will not be a man that will use my authority and power over my wife but love her for who she is **(Genesis 3:16).** Give me ears to hear the cry and groan of my wife. Give me ears to hear You clearly concerning my wife and children. Give me eyes to perceive when there is a problem in my marriage. Give me a heart to support my wife in all circumstances.

Give my wife fortune and treasure that will bring a blessing not sorrow. Reward her labour of love and let her be a precious gift to me. Give her a name that will be recognised worldwide. Give her a business that will produce lasting fruit and make God's name great. Race, gender, ethnic minority will not be a hindrance to increase my wife. Give her a breakthrough that will wipe away her sorrow and tears, blessing that will take away her reproach, shame, guilt and disgrace, give her beauty for ashes, the oil of joy for mourning, garments of praise for the spirit of heaviness **(Isaiah 61:2-3).**

I will make our anniversaries a memorial to the lord. To thank God for another year that we get to spend together and to invite the Lord to reside in our marriage for the years to come. In this celebration between me and my wife, I will re- affirm our love, covenant and commitment for one another. Things that are working well and not working so well will be placed before the Lord and ask for wisdom and understanding. Above all we will seal our covenant/celebration by praying and breaking communion.

HUSBAND

What is a man's biblical role as a husband? **The husband should fulfil his marital duty to his wife, and likewise the wife to her husband. The wife does not have authority over her own body but yields it to her husband. In the same way, the husband does not have authority over his own body but yields it to his wife. Do not deprive each other except perhaps by mutual consent and for a time, so that you may devote yourselves to prayer. Then come together again so that Satan will not tempt you because of your lack of self-control. I say this as a concession, not as a command. I wish that all of you were as I am. But each of you has your own gift from God; one has this gift, another has that. (1 Corinthians 7:3-7).**

I want us to look at the keywords in the above scripture. What do they mean? **Fulfil**: achieve, and desire to carry out your role to satisfy and meet the marital duty to your wife. **Authority:** You have the power or right to give orders and make decisions on behalf of both of you. **Yield:** Make yourself available and provide, for your wife. **Deprive:** Do not prevent your wife from having what she deserves. There is no such thing as I am not in the mood or I do not want to have sex because you upset me or you did not give me what I asked for. This is not right and God will not be pleased with you. **Consent**: Marriage is a partnership. Even though you are the head of the home, your wife has permission in building your home just like you. **Devote:** Be a husband that gives your time to pray and intercede for your wife. **Self-control**:

Be a man who is able to restrain himself. Lack of self-control will destroy your home. While in some homes it can be forgiven and life goes on, it is not that simple in some marriages and can lead to divorce. **Gift:** You have a natural ability or talent from God which will bless both of you, you do not need to be jealous/ envious/ threatened / feel inferior due to your wife's gifts. You are one and working together to build a home. What are your thoughts as you read the above? I will leave this with you to digest and ponder. The secrets of a lasting marriage depend on both the husband and wife working together. It is not only the money in the bank account, houses or cars you possess that make a good and lasting marriage but looking beyond your wife's attitude towards you, complimenting her, covering her shame and weaknesses. Bring the best out of her, ignore her nagging and focus on her strength. It is ironic that Paul used Christ and the Church to describe the role of a man. He could have said husbands love your wives and stop there but he wanted us to understand it is more than that. God sees the bigger picture and He is coming back for His bride. So, your home is not just your own but the Lord's.

Husbands, love your wives, just as Christ loved the church and gave himself up for her to make her holy, cleansing her by the washing with water through the word, and to present her to himself as a radiant church, without stain or wrinkle or any other blemish, but holy and blameless. In this same way, husbands ought to love their wives as their own bodies. He who loves his wife loves himself. After all, no one ever hated their own

body, but they feed and care for their body, just as Christ does the church— for we are members of his body. "For this reason a man will leave his father and mother and be united to his wife, and the two will become one flesh." This is a profound mystery—but I am talking about Christ and the church. However, each one of you also must love his wife as he loves himself, and the wife must respect her husband. (Ephesians5:25-33). My understanding of the above scripture is that husbands should love their wife as Christ loves the church and must be willing to sacrifice their life for her. 1 corinthians13:4-7 explains that the kind of love husbands must have towards their wife should be patient, kind, always protecting, always trusting, always hopes and perseveres. Love must not envy nor boast, nor be proud. It does not dishonour, self-seeking, easily angered and it keeps no record of wrongs. The kind of love the Lord requires from you does not delight in evil but rejoices with the truth. If you adopt this kind of love in your marriage, you will have a long and satisfying marriage. Husbands must be willing to look beyond their wife's weaknesses. Forgive even before the wife offends them. Be part of the process of washing away her dirty linen through the word of God instead of exposing her weaknesses. Present your wife to the world with dignity, respect and honour. Remember she is the bone of your bones and the flesh of your flesh. What you do affects her and what she does will affect you. You are both one in Christ and both of you are unique to your Father.

Create regular time together to talk about your marriage. I heard an inspirational message recently about taking 'One day at a time' by Ben Bluemel. In the message Ben explained how important it is for a husband and wife to spend time together regularly not on one big holiday but consistent and daily communion with each other (Hillsong UK podcast 2/6/2020). Communication is one of the key instruments in marriages. If you get it right your home will be fine. It is important to talk to your wife. I heard that some men are not talkers. As much as I disagree with this I also leave a small window of truth to the fact that it can be an individual's personality but you cannot go into marriage without communicating with the person you are living with. The reason I disagree with this is because, while you were courting/dating each other you did talk to this lady and then after marriage you decided to switch off because of reasons like 'she nags a lot, we do not share the same views, the lady at my office understand me better, she does not get me, the children get in the way'. I do understand those who are not much of a talker before marriage and now that they are married, the wife is making an issue out of it. You must find the best way to communicate with your wife in order to have continuous peace in your marriage. You are as important as well as your wife in this marriage. So make most of it. What you put in will determine what you will get from it. Find a communication system that works for both of you. For example, know the best time to talk about issues. Some people tend to talk about issues while it is fresh in their mind while others tend to wait, think about it and find out when to bring up the subject. Some bottle up their concerns because they do not think the other person can handle it, but you are not doing yourself a favour by bottling your concerns, it will only make matters worse. If you think your wife will not be able to handle what you want to share with her, take it to your heavenly Father who knows and can do all things. Let the Holy Spirit help you to communicate what is on your heart to your wife effectively in order to strengthen your marriage. **If any of you lacks wisdom, let him ask of God, who gives to all liberally and without reproach, and it will be given to him. (James1:5)**

Also, do not assume that your wife will not understand what you are going through or she will not be able to handle the situation. Majority of men have gotten themselves into trouble by not sharing information with their wife. You may be the head of the family but you are not there to carry the entire burden on your shoulder, your wife is there to help you. Learn how to lead your home the way our Lord Jesus led his disciples. Though He was the head of the church, He made Himself available to them, taught them, shared their pain and in return they made sure He was fed. For instance, if a bill needs to be paid for and you are struggling to pay it, tell your wife. It is better to bring her into the situation as she might know a way out. You are not alone in your marriage, you have a helper. Learn to be vulnerable with your wife. You are doing yourself a favour when you love her as you love yourself. Hence, a man needs to experience true love himself in order to be able to give it. You can only give what you have. This is why it is important to figure out who you are, where you are going and what you want to do with your life before you invite another person in to come and share it with you. The bible says in **Habakkuk2:2** to write the vision and make it plain so that those who read it, will have clarity about where you are going. People perish without clear direction. Your actions are what will make your marriage last a lifetime. If you are already married, it is not too late to reflect now and make a decision to be a good husband.

Do not listen to the lies of the devil in regards to your wife or children. Treat your wife well so that your prayers can be answered. I cannot understand how a husband can sleep at night when the wife is hurting. Can you sleep when you are in pain? You claim to love this wife but you not willing to share in her pain. I have prayer partners that I sometimes feel like they are in my house when I am going through something. When the phone rings and they share what is on their mind it is as if I have told them about it already.

It is the Husband's responsibility to study and understand his wife. Jesus always perceived what was going on in men's hearts **(Luke5:22, Mark2:8, Matthew 12:25)** and if you want to love like Jesus you have to perceive what is going on with your wife. **Husbands, in the same way be considerate as you live with your wives, and treat them with respect as the weaker partner and as heirs with you of the gracious gift of life, so that nothing will hinder your prayers.(1 Peter 3:7)**

Do not be a lazy husband rather choose to be hardworking and do your best to take care of your family. Finance is an area that affects marriages and breaks homes. It is the man's responsibility to make sure that your finances are secure and to manage the resources the Lord has given to you. I understand that in some homes responsibilities are shared and situations do arise i.e. job loss, redundancy or the business collapses. Do not hide your struggles from your wife, problems can be solved quickly when shared. There is a saying that a problem shared is a problem solved. Adam and Eve were naked but not ashamed **(Genesis2:25KJV)**. Do not leave two people's responsibility for one person to carry, it will only bring strain, separation and probably divorce. Do all you can to be transparent. Let your wife know what you are doing and what is going on in your life. Years ago, I nearly lost a friend who later helped me in a very difficult season of life, just because I could not express what was going on with me or I thought she would not understand. If there is a problem do not hide it from your wife, face it and solve it together. **You lazy fool, look at an ant. Watch it closely; let it teach you a thing or two. Nobody has to tell it what to do. All summer it stores up food; at harvest it stockpiles provisions. So how long are you going to laze around doing nothing? How long before you get out of bed? A nap here, a nap there, a day off here, a day off there, sit back, take it easy—do you know what comes next? Just this: You can look forward to a dirt-poor life, poverty your permanent houseguest! (Proverbs6:6-11MSG)**

Avoid taking for granted an opportunity that comes your way. Do not be a man that takes advantage of government resources. The fact that you are supported to get back on your feet, does not give you the right to stay there, it deprives others who genuinely need help to access the same fund. This behaviour is inconsiderate and selfish. If you are able, physically fit and have the mental ability to work, get out there and find a job to feed your family. There are so many people who are desperate to receive these kinds of privileges and it's wrong for anyone to misuse public funds. Let our behaviour reflect the image of the Father who created us and gave us dominion over all that he made. **Riffraff and rascals talk out of both sides of their mouths. They wink at each other, they shuffle their feet, they cross their fingers behind their backs. Their perverse minds are always cooking up something nasty, always stirring up trouble. Catastrophe is just around the corner for them, a total smash up, their lives ruined beyond repair. There are Seven Things God Hates and they are: he who loathes with a passion: eyes that are arrogant, a tongue that lies, hands that murder the innocent, a heart that hatches evil plots, feet that race down a wicked track, a mouth that lies under oath, a troublemaker in the family. (Proverbs 6:16-19MSG).**

The devil is not a respecter of person, the fact that you have been married for several years does not mean you are out of the enemy's radar. Remember he roams about looking for who he will devour, let it not be your home **(1Peter5:8)**. Do not lose your guard in regards to everything that concerns you especially your home. Stay faithful to the wife of your youth. Do not be deceived by the devil that it is greener outside your home and another woman is better than your wife. No one can take the place of your wife, she is your helper and your companion till death do you part. Even your children cannot replace your wife. Many might be better than her but none can satisfy you better than her. How would you feel if someone says he/she does not like your face or part of your body? This is exactly what happens when you defile your matrimonial bed. You are telling your wife she is worthless, she is no good and above all your action brings foul smell into God's presence and your prayer will not be answered. **Dear friend, do what I tell you; treasure my careful instructions. Do what I say and you'll live well. My teaching is as precious as your eyesight—guard it! Write it out on the back of your hands; etch it on the chambers of your heart. Talk to Wisdom as to a sister. Treat Insight as your companion. They'll be with you to fend off the Temptress—that smooth-talking, honey-tongued Seductress. (Proverbs 7:1-5MSG).** I read Luke 12 one morning for my devotion. It was about not being afraid of those who can only kill my body but to be afraid of the one who has the authority to kill me and throw my body in hell. There are consequences for disobeying God and if you think your wife cannot see what you are doing, there is one who sees everything in the secret and He will bring it to the open soon. The Lord loves your wife and listens to her cry. The pain of not being loved rises to heaven and in due course, He will avenge her cause and turn her captivity into freedom.

As I stood at the window of my house looking out through the shutters, watching the mindless crowd stroll by, I spotted a young man without any sense arriving at the corner of the street where she lived, then turning up the path to her house. It was dusk, the evening coming on, the darkness thickening into night. Just then, a woman met

him— she'd been lying in wait for him, dressed to seduce him. Brazen and brash she was, restless and roaming, never at home, walking the streets, loitering in the mall, hanging out at every corner in town. She threw her arms around him and kissed him, boldly took his arm and said, "I've got all the makings for a feast— today I made my offerings, my vows are all paid, So now I've come to find you, hoping to catch sight of your face—and here you are! I've spread fresh, clean sheets on my bed, colourful imported linens. My bed is aromatic with spices and exotic fragrances. Come, let's make love all night, spend the night in ecstatic lovemaking! My husband's not home; he's away on business, and he won't be back for a month." Soon she has him eating out of her hand, bewitched by her honeyed speech. Before you know it, he's trotting behind her, like a calf led to the butcher shop, like a stag lured into ambush and then shot with an arrow, Like a bird flying into a net not knowing that its flying life is over. So, friends, listen to me, take these words of mine most seriously. Don't fool around with a woman like that; don't even stroll through her neighbourhood. Countless victims come under her spell; she's the death of many a poor man. She runs a halfway house to hell, fits you out with a shroud and a coffin. (Proverbs 7:6-27)

I am not saying marriage is easy but it is worth throwing all you have into it and keeping it. Stay away from the other woman who is coming to steal your joy, kill your peace and destroy your home. Love, cherish and honour your wife and this blessing will come to you. A wife of noble character who can find? She is worth far more than rubies. Her husband has full confidence in her and lacks nothing of value .he brings him good, not harm, all the days of her life. She selects wool and flax and works with eager hands. She is like the merchant ships, bringing her food from afar. She gets up while it is still night; she provides food for her family and portions for her female servants. She considers a field and buys it; out of her earnings she plants a vineyard. She sets about her work vigorously; her arms are strong for her tasks. She sees that her trading is profitable, and her lamp does not go out at night. In her hand she holds the distaff and grasps the spindle with her fingers. She opens her arms to the poor and extends her hands to the needy. When it snows, she has no fear for her household; for all of them are clothed in scarlet. She makes coverings for her bed; she is clothed in fine linen and purple. Her husband is respected at the city gate, where he takes his seat among the elders of the land. She makes linen garments and sells them, and supplies the merchants with sashes. She is clothed with strength and dignity; she can laugh at the days to come. She speaks with wisdom, and faithful instruction is on her tongue. She watches over the affairs of her household and does not eat the bread of idleness. Her children arise and call her blessed; her husband also, and he praises her: "Many women do noble things, but you surpass them all." Charm is deceptive, and beauty is fleeting; but a woman who fears the Lord is to be praised. Honour her for all that her hands have done, and let her works

bring her praise at the city gate. (Proverbs31:10-31).

PRAYER AND CONFESSION

Thank God for the privilege of becoming a husband

I will love my wife as Christ loved the Church and gave His life for it.

I will cherish my wife all the days of my life and will not allow anything to come between us. I will honour and esteem her for she is worth more than gold and silver

I receive the wisdom to fulfil my role as a husband. I receive knowledge and understanding to treat my wife the way of God. I receive discretion to protect me from the schemes of the devil. I receive the spirit of discernment to perceive when my wife is hurting and give me wisdom to act accordingly **(Daniel2:20-22)**

I will receive wise counsel; every counsel to have an affair, abuse my wife or defile my matrimonial bed I will not yield to it.

I receive wisdom to sow and reap great harvest. I will not deprive my wife of the right she deserved. I will be devoted to my wife

I will shower my wife with precious gifts constantly not just on special occasion

Pride/arrogance/ego will not be in the way of consent. I will not misuse the authority God has given me as a husband. I receive the spirit of self-control and discipline at all times

Deliver me from temptation, from a promiscuous and adulterous woman. I will not treat other women better than my wife

I will treat my wife the way I would like to be treated. I disallow anything that will cause my wife any stress. I allow everything that will bring peace, joy, love, endurance, tolerance in my marriage

My marriage is planted by the river of flowing waters. My marriage will flourish, heaven will rain plenty and kindness to my marriage **(Act14:17).**

The success of my marriage will nourish many **(Proverb10:21).** I incline and apply wisdom in my marriage **(proverbs 2:1-11),** no good thing will I lack in my marriage. I receive every good gift from heaven **(Psalms 84:11)**

In health and wholeness I will enjoy my marriage and my wife. My wife and I will live long and be satisfied **(Psalm91:16)** I will not speak evil about my wife rather my words will be pleasant, pure, true, honourable, praiseworthy, peaceful, worthy of respect **(Philippians4:8-9)**

I will have wisdom that is greater than the Wisdom of Solomon to govern my marriage **(Matthew12:42)**

1 Chronicles16:22 says touch not my anointed and do my prophet no harm. Everyone that rises against my marriage will be condemned **Deuteronomy28:7.** The Lord will raise a standard against anyone that wants to destroy my home **(Isaiah59:19)**

I receive the mystery in my marriage **(Daniel 2:23).** I receive wisdom to obtain knowledge of what is going on in my marriage. I refuse to be illiterate, foolish, oblivious and ignorant to the needs in my marriage

I receive the wisdom that comes from heaven which is pure, peace loving, considerate, submissive, full of mercy, good fruit, impartial and sincere towards my wife **(James3:17).** My intentions will be based on the word of God

I will pay attention to the instruction and principles laid down in the scripture for my marriage to succeed

FATHER

It is a privilege and honour for a marriage to be blessed with children. The bible says children are a blessing **(Psalms 127:3-5).** They do not complete your marriage but for sure they enhance it. It is joyful and beautiful to be called a father. If you are still waiting to be a father and it has not happened yet, hold on to God and believe that He who has promised is able to give you a child one day. **"But you—you serve your God and he'll bless your food and your water. I'll get rid of the sickness among you; there won't be any miscarriages nor barren women in your land. I'll make sure you live full and complete lives". (Exodus23:25-26MSG**). It is important that the husband and wife know and understand what they want in regards to children. Consider these questions together; do you want children? How many? Sometimes, due to medical complications some men or women cannot have children. In this case, work together with your wife to come up with the solution that best suit your marriage.

There are many options while you are waiting. You can adopt, foster or help a woman struggling to send her children to school or feed her children. There is no shame in bringing a child who is not your own into your home as long as it is in agreement with your wife. It is important to know that if you are not able to give your wife a child it is not a sign of weakness or failure as a man. When Rachel asked Jacob to give him children or she will die, Jacob referred her back to her maker **(Genesis 30:2).** If you decide to adopt, it is an answered prayer to one of God's children. Pray and talk to your wife about it and make a joint decision on the issue so that in the future there is no blame game like Adam and Eve. The Lord delights when we give freedom to the captive and provide a Godly home for a child. The bible says out of the mouth of babies the Lord ordained praise **(Psalms8:2)**. How do you think a father feels when he sees his children mistreated and suffering on one end and on another end there is a man who is able to help but refuses to? The Lord will not come down from heaven, He needs human beings to execute His justice on earth. Babies are neglected daily because they are not wanted, or the parent has died or is not capable of taking care of the child. Many babies are suffering and need a loving home. Babies are being trafficked all over the world. Choose to make a difference. There are reasons why people cannot agree to bring another child into their home i.e. finances, issues in the home, space, what will people say. If finances are the reason, ask God to provide and show you in what capacity He wants you to help. He did say He will give us the desires of our hearts. I and my boys sponsor a beautiful girl called Yeisy with the little finance God has given us. To me, the amount we send may not be much but to her and her family it buys her new clothes, pays for her to go to school and gives her a chance to know God. How awesome is that? My baby is now in secondary school, growing and loving life and I believe one day we will see each other.

There is no pressure if it is your desire not to have children or bring a child into your home. I believe God honours your decision. I am just bringing awareness to those who want to do something while waiting but do not know how to go about it. I am not an expert on the subject but if you and your wife agree to adopt, do your homework very well and make sure it is through a reputable organisation. Do not play a part in child trafficking. In agreement, pray about what child will be suitable for your home in terms of age and sex. It is important that the conversation comes from men regardless of where the complication of childbearing comes from and I will tell you why. Wives need the support of their husband to fulfil this desire. It is a huge step and it will need the support of each other. I have seen couples where the wife welcomes the idea and is passionate about it but the husband does not want to hear or even consider it. When your wife brings out the subject about adoption or any other form of helping children in care/motherless homes, listen to her, let her know you are with her. Let her know that you understand where she is coming from and you are willing to support her. She has put a lot of thoughts and emotions into this and it will hurt if you dismiss her without any consideration whatsoever. Think about it even if it is not something that interests you and give her an alternative that both of you will agree on. In that case at least she knows she has your support and you can explore different options together. This is not the time for you to wander off and invite the devil into your home or get angry or get defensive when the topic comes up. Above all commit your plan into the hands of God and He will bring it to pass **(Psalm 37:5).** If you already have children of your own, it is fair to consider the option your wife puts forward to you especially if she has never had children. Work with her and come alongside her to bring it to reality.

When I said 'option', I do not mean the one that Abraham agreed to do by listening to Sarah to sleep with Hagar and the story did not end well **(Genesis16)**. Or when Lea and Rachel gave their servants to Jacob to sleep with. Jacob's desire for one woman he loved ended up with four wives **(Genesis30)**. Always put your concerns before the Lord. The bible says cast all your cares upon him for he cares for you **(1Peter5:7)**. There are no problems that God cannot solve. Jesus said, **"Come to me, all you who are weary and burdened, and I will give you rest. Take my yoke upon you and learn from me, for I am gentle and humble in heart, and you will find rest for your souls. For my yoke is easy and my burden is light." (Matthew11:28-30)**. I pray that the Lord will lead you to do the right thing and make the right decision when it comes to adopting, fostering, sponsoring and helping a child or family in need.

Now let us dive into the responsibility of a father. Not every biological father is capable of becoming a good father. It is the responsibility of both parents to train up their children/ child in the way of the lord. Regardless of your circumstances whether you live with the child or not it is your duty to provide for the child you brought into the world. There are some instances whereby you are cut off from the child, do whatever you can do in your power to maintain contact with the child and provide for the child welfare. Open a trust fund in the child's name until you are able to connect with the child. I must say I am one of the most fortunate single mum whose ex-husband helps when he can to support and care for his children. Life is tough, so is bringing up a child/children alone with no support from the other parent. It is sad that majority of problems around the world are caused by absent fathers and I am not being sexist here. We cannot under estimate the role of a man in the home. While some may disagree with me on this, I still feel strongly that the void of a man in a home cannot always be rectified by a woman alone, it needs both the man and woman that is why God created mankind- male and female. While many will say that some men do not live to the expectation in the home which concludes that men are not needed in the home, I disagree! As much as women try to fill the gap/ mend the brokenness caused by absent fathers, it is important to know that only the person who made the hole can fix it. When do things turn peer shaped in the home? When the home is divided, when girls become dad's favourite and boys become mum's favourite. The bible says the house divided against itself will not stand **(Mark3:25, Matthew12:25-28).** Where in the bible do you see a father preferring a daughter to a son? It is the culture of this world and it needs to change.

Every child needs their father in their life and I believe boys need their father more to show them what life was like when the Dad was growing up. Fathers need to rise to this challenge and help their boys become the men they are created to be. **Proverb22:6** instructs us to train up a child in the way to go and when he is old will not depart from it. There is some information a woman will give a child that will not be enough even with the help of google. Be available and be part of bringing up your children. In my opinion boys should be the closest to their father. Majority of anger and violence experienced by men may have come from having no role model while growing up. Let us look at this in God's perspective. He is our Father and He has shown us countless of scriptures about who He is and who He wants us to be in the world. If He made us in His image and likeness we ought to live up to that image. We saw His relationship between Him and His son. Jesus always referred to His Father wherever He went. There is a saying in my language that says; charity begins at home. Parents/guardians must remember that the cute little boy will become a man one day and it is their responsibility to train, equip and support the boy's emotion, spiritual, intellect, moral, mental being/development. The world is full of many characters and changes and it is important to channel the children into the right direction. As parents, we need to constantly educate ourselves about these changes and help our children in any way we can to understand the world around them. Do not leave your responsibilities to the mother or family members. Find out what works best for both parents to meet the needs of the children. For example, in some homes it is the man who helps with the children's education while the wife concentrates on their welfare. In another home it is the father that does the cooking while the mother focuses on the child's education. Find what your strengths are and utilise them in your home. The greatest mistake is to think that your contribution is not useful/valued/needed. Your wife/partner/ mother of your child is not your enemy, the devil is. I have heard or seen men demonstrate their gift and interest with friends outside the home but refuse to let the wife/partner know. Your education, experience, knowledge, childhood memory, understanding, fun memories, successes, failures are all part of the tool a child needs to manoeuver his/her environment. Share any information you know whether relevant or not to help the children to understand the discipline and advice you are trying to convey to them. I have a family friend who fascinates me. When their children were young they decided to home school them so the wife who was a midwife gave up her job to look after their five children while the husband continued to work to provide for the family. The five children did very well and ended up in universities and even did masters. Now the children are all grown up and the mother can do whatever she wants to do. Communication is vital when bringing up children, each party has something to give and their life experience has an important part in the children's life.

There are many things I would not be able to write with regards to bringing up a child i.e. bereavement, loss of a wife, step mom or children and extended family. Being a father is a huge responsibility which is not taught in college or university or homes unless you step into it but great reward awaits fathers who commit to it till the end. If there is a complication or barrier between you and your child, seek good counsel and allow the Holy Spirit to help you. It encourages me when my ex-husband gives me compliments and acknowledges that I take care of our boys. Make yourself visible in the life of your child. If you are not allowed to see the child, create an account for the child and deposit funds, write letters, birthday cards even if you have no address to post them to. Fight for your child in a peaceful manner. Do all you can for the day the child will show up at your doorstep and you can let him/her know you did your best. I do know that some women do exploit the goodness/generosity of some fathers but I pray that God will give you wisdom and strength **(Proverbs8:14).**

The father and child relationship is the one demonstrated by God Himself when He created mankind in His image **(Genesis1:27)** and sent His son to die for humanity. This was to show us that He cares for us deeply. Jesus also helped us to know who God is by showing us the relationship with His Father. He never did anything without consulting His father. When He was weary before His death, He talked to the Father **(Matthew27:46)**. Jesus always referred to God as His Father which makes Christianity different to other religions. As a father, you should love your children as God loves you and show no partiality between your children. Our God is the Lord of Lords who shows no partiality between His children. If He does, only Jewish people will be able to enter the kingdom of God but He tore the veil and gave all humanity the opportunity to come to Him **(Matthew27:51).** The relationship with your child should be the one you pay attention to and invite the one who is the best in parenting (God) to help you. You need the wisdom of God to direct and guide you **(Proverb2:10-11).**

It is a privilege and an honour to be counted worthy to be a father. Treat it with gentleness, meekness, kindness and love. Remember that you are only a guardian, God is their Father and you will give account on how you look after His child/children. Children are a blessing from the Lord, regardless of what you think about them. They are a gift from the Lord and a reward from Him. Do not misuse the authority that God has given you as the head of the family and as a father, to exploit or control your children, it will only create a barrier, bitterness, resentment, un-forgiveness and hatred. The bible says, fathers, do not exasperate your children; instead, bring them up in the training and instruction of the Lord **(Ephesians 6:4)**. Jesus used a child to describe humility and who qualifies to enter His kingdom **(Matthew18:2-5)**. Children will try your patience, get on your nerves, manipulate and use different tactics to get what they want. It is your responsibility to stand firm and discipline them in the way of God. Many times the Holy Spirit has reminded me that I am the parent and I have to discipline my children. The bible says, those who spare the rod hate their children and those who love their children will carefully discipline them **(Proverbs13:24)**. Depending on which part of the world you are reading this book from, the bible always tells us to follow the rule of the land. You have to ask yourself whether beating/ smacking a child will achieve the same result as talking to her/him. Think about yourself for a moment, how do you think God corrects you? Through judgement or discipline? The bible also says, who the father loves he corrects **(Hebrews12:6)**. Whatever you do make sure it is done and received with love. Eli heard about what his children were doing but did not rebuke them and the position that was meant for his children was given to Samuel **(1Samuel2:12-36)**. David ignored the behaviour of his children and it resulted in one raping his sister **(2Samuel13:1-27)**, one killing his brother **(2Samuel13:28-39)**, one fought with his father for kingship position and **(2Samuel15-17)** one tried to undermine his father by declaring himself king while his father was still on the throne **(1King1:6),** and one decided to kill everyone in his father's house. There are consequences for not training our children in the way they should go.

However, do not discipline your children to suit your own agenda or to get back at your wife/exe/partner. Do not use your children to achieve your own goals or to make a point, it will bounce back to hurt you. Jesus talked about what will happen to those who offend their children **(Matthew18:6, 10)**. Be careful of what you do or say to your children so that your prayers are not hindered. You do not want to curse what God has blessed. If you are asking a question about how to be a father to your children, I think the best place to start is to find out your relationship with your heavenly Father and then gradually ask yourself the following questions: Who is my biological father? What is my adopted father like? Do I really know my father? What is the story about my father? Is he an absent or present father? (this does not necessarily mean whether he lives with you or not). What are the good and bad memories of my father? What is the story about grandad? Was I raised by a step father, brother, uncle, aunties? Who is a father figure in my life? Who do I look up to? Who is my role model? Where do I get counsel in regards to my child or home? What is my understanding of a father? After answering those questions if you feel angry, upset, defensive, happy, mixed feelings, then the question now is what will you do about how you feel? I am not a psychologist or family advocate but if you feel the way you relate to your children is not the way you should, then seek advice from the appropriate professionals and ask the Holy Spirit to lead you. However, if you have lost your way as a father, the previous chapters will take you back to who God created you to be.

The reason I asked you to think about these questions is not to degrade you as a father but for you to reflect on where you are coming from and what changes you want to make in regards to your child/children. Let me tell you a little bit of my relationship with my dad. We lived together until I was 11, then my parents divorced so I had to go and live with my mum but I could still visit my dad whenever he was available. I do not remember having a close relationship with him. He was in his 50s when I was born so that did not help as he always saw me as a little girl even though I grew taller than him when he was alive. My attitude as I was growing up was I did not need him as my mother catered for all my needs but when I got married and started having problems in my marriage, I began to feel his absence even though I do not know him. I would cry for him whenever something happened between me and my husband. I do not know what I was crying for because if he was alive, I do not think that I would have called him to tell him the issues in my home. At one point in my marriage, I was really struggling to understand God and my connect group leader at the time asked me what my relationship with my father was like. I think I got offended and probably defensive plus angry as I did not see the relevance of the question. Ignoring my reaction she proceeded and said maybe I was using my experience with my biological father to relate to the heavenly Father. This got me thinking. I believed that the God I have known for over 30 years was a distant God not a Father that is present. The God I knew was I didn't want to have a close relationship with. Part of me wanted Him but another part of me thought He would disappoint me like my earthly father. I had created this relationship whereby I was alone and I made decisions based on that attitude. This reflection helped me realise that the God I thought I knew wasn't my heavenly Father and I had to reconnect with Him. It turned my life around, even though my marriage ended, it helped me to maintain a good relationship with the father of my children, which is important to me and mostly important to God. I will ask the question again: What is your relationship with God? If you have lost your connection with God, this is the moment to pause, ask Him to forgive you and ask Him to come into your life. He is always at the door of your heart and He is happy to have you back. Invite Him today and you will not regret it. If you have offended your biological father, humble yourself and apologise. If your father has offended you, forgive him for he know not what he did. As you have noticed in your parenting skills, there are some things you will get right and somethings you will get wrong. Find it in your heart to forgive your parent for that is your leverage to a happy life. The bible says honour your parent so that it will be well with you **(Deuteronomy5:16).** One area where mankind struggles with in life is neglecting or dishonouring parents. **Proverbs23:22** says, listen to your father, who gave you life, and do not despise your mother when she is old. May you be the father that God is pleased with a Father like Abraham who was not happy when his son had to move away from him, God had to assure him that He would bless Ishmael before he could let go **(Genesis21:11-14)**.

PRAYER AND CONFESSION: For those waiting to be a father

I thank God in advance for the opportunity to carry my own child

Every complication hindering child bearing is cancelled with the blood of Jesus. I will testify of God's goodness for the promised child. Everything interfering in me bearing a child, whether medically, spiritually, mentally or psychologically, I cancel it with the blood of Jesus. I will sing for joy for my quiver will be full of children **(Psalms127:5)**. While waiting, I will not confess anything that is negative even if I have not seen the manifestation of my prayers yet.

The Lord Almighty has sworn, **"Surely, as I have planned, so it will be, and as I have purposed, so it will happen. I will crush the Assyrian in my land; on my mountains I will trample him down. His yoke will be taken from my people, and his burden removed from their shoulders. "This is the plan determined for the whole world; this is the hand stretched out over all nations. For the Lord Almighty has purposed, and who can thwart him? His hand is stretched out, and who can turn it back? (Isaiah14:24-27).** The plan and purpose of God for my marriage will stand, no evil will thwart it. I trample and crush every plot, plan and scheme of the evil one. All generational curses of barrenness in my family or my wife's family from 10th generations are broken by the blood of Jesus Christ. Any evil words spoken over my life or on behalf of my life and my wife will be nullified by the blood of Jesus. The blood of Jesus speaks for us. The blood that death sees and pass over, that blood makes childlessness pass over me. I reject pre-mature pregnancy. My wife and I will not lose any child that God will give to us. God has the final say over our life not the doctors. I believe the report of the Lord and declare His report will come to reality in Jesus's name,

My wife and I confess and ask God to forgive us for our ignorance, cohabiting, sex before marriage, adultery, unfaithfulness. Create a clean heart in us and renew a right spirit within us **(Psalms51:10-12).**

As Jabez prayed and you granted his request and expanded his territory, Oh God I pray that you will bless my marriage with children **(1Chronicles4:9-10).** Enlarge our territory

If I have done, said, imagined anything that has caused a delay, I repent and declare God's promise in **Exodus23:26** that I will not be barren and my wife will not suffer miscarriage. Any delay will work for my good and according to His purpose **(Romans8:28).** I know delays are not denials, though it tarries I will surely wait for it because I know that Your promise never fails **(Revelation21:4).**

Abraham was old when he had Isaac **(Genesis21:5).** Age will not be a barrier to be productive. As Isaac prayed for his wife to bear children **(Genesis25:21),** so I pray for my wife to bear children.

Your declaration for us to be fruitful, multiply and fill the earth will come to pass in my life. The God that made the Heavens and the earth by His great power and outstretched arm is able to give me a child and I know there is nothing too hard for Him **(Jeremiah 32:17).**

Children the Lord will give to me will be like arrows in a warrior's hand **(Psalms127:4).** My children will be wise and make me proud and turn out well in life **(Proverbs23:24).** Wise children that will reverence and honour God. Children like Samuel who became the first prophet **(1 Samuel3:19-21),** Solomon who build a house for God **(1 King 9:1-2),** children who covered the shame and nakedness of their father **(Genesis9:23).**

God open my eyes to see and hear Your intentions for my marriage. If You want me to adopt or foster, may I embrace it. Your word says you will not give me what I cannot handle and when You do, You will provide a way out so that I can endure it **(1 Corinthians10:13). King James version of the same scripture says,** He will make a way to escape in order to be able to bear it **(paraphrased). TPT version says He will provide escape that will bring me out victoriously.** My story will end victoriously.

I will not allow what people say determine my actions to foster/adopt. I will not let selfishness rob me of the blessings God will bring through looking after someone else's children. God will be the drive behind my actions. I will not listen to the voice of doubt or fear. My adopted/fostered children will bring reward and blessings not regret and disgrace.

PRAYER/CONFESSION: Father

Thank God for the opportunity to be a father and the children God gave you.

I ask for wisdom to guide and train my child in your way **(James1:5)**. I ask for wisdom to make decisions regarding my children. My choices will not hinder the plan that You have for them **(Luke18:16)**. My life will be a reflection of who You are Lord, and I will not make my children to turn away from You. My attitude and behaviour will not make them to hate God or want nothing to do with God.

Favouritism brings division, hatred and even death if it gets out of hand. Isaac thought he was helping Esau by telling him to prepare food for him so that he could give him his last blessing but Rebekah sabotaged the conversation. Jacob received his brother's blessing and ended up running for his life **(Genesis27)**. I will not try to help God by my actions and turn that which is meant for good into a disaster. Jacob's love for Joseph more than the rest of his children because he was born in his old age did not help Joseph instead it made his brothers to hate him more. I will not create rivalry between my children.

(Ephesians 6:4), I will not provoke my children but nurture them. Even when a child thinks I do not love him/her. I will make it my responsibility to correct and assure the child that he/she is loved.

I will not be a barrier to my children's progress and success but a bridge that leads them to their destiny. I will not prefer a child to another. It is not scriptural as I do not see it in my heavenly Father's character **(Deuteronomy7:7-8).**

I will not bring division or enmity between my children **(Romans2:11).** The enemy will not steal, kill and destroy their joy and peace.

I will love/treat my children equally and respect their views, opinion and decisions. Lord, I will not use my hand to destroy the destiny of my son. I will not crush their manhood and the potential that is in them **(Acts 10:34-35).** I disallow hatred between my children and speak peace and harmony between them. They will not take their frustration or anger on each other.

When things are not going on well for one of my children the other will step in to help, give strength and support, love, care for him/her. My children will listen, empower and encourage each other. Nothing will come between their friendship and love for each other.

The covenant between David and Jonathan was established until death and even after death, Melphibosheth - Jonathan's son reap from that covenant **(2Samuel 9).** I pray that my children will not only be brother/sisters but covenant friends. May he/she be content, satisfied with who they are and what they have.

I reject the spirit of envy, jealousy, evil/ negative thoughts towards each other. When my child comes to me for advice, my advice will not be motivated by my own selfish desires. I will give advice based on the intuition of the Holy Spirit. My words will align with the plan God has for he/her life and I will support, embrace, trust and respect their decisions **(Romans8:26-27)**.

Father, give me wisdom, understanding and listening ears to solve conflicts between my children. Give me insight to reconcile differences that may arise between my children. I choose to be a peace maker. I declare patience, endurance and tolerance when dealing with unresolved issues in our family.

May the Lord's peace reign in our conversations as we solve problems and deal with situations in my home. Lord, heal the one that is hurt and upset. Comfort the one who is broken during misunderstandings. Help us to understand each other when we come together to resolve conflict.

May we not allow or listen to the one whose aim is to steal, kill and destroy our family. Every plot of the evil one to divide my children will not stand in Jesus's name. I reject the spirit of bitterness, resentment, unforgiveness and rebellion in Jesus's name **(Ephesians 4:26. Luke17:3-4)**.

EMPLOYEE

If you are employed then this chapter is for you. In this chapter you will learn the biblical principles applicable you as an employee. When the offer of employment letter is received, there are different thoughts that go through people's mind depending on how long they have been waiting for a job. Perhaps you are given a job you did not deserve or did not do well in the interview or thousands applied and only you qualified for the position. The feeling is amazing and an answer to long awaited prayers. Few days later you are invited for an induction. This is the day you will be told when to start work and what you will be doing. The company will give you the policy and procedures, and the required training you will need to help you understand the job. As the company presents you with their policy and procedures, I am also presenting you with God's word. This will help you to understand God's mind in regards to your workplace. There is a blessing when we do things God's way. What will be covered in this chapter might be the answer to the questions you have been asking or struggling with all these is years. When we follow Godly principles, curses, lack and failure has no place in our life. Let us look at what the scriptures say: **Slaves, obey your earthly masters with respect and fear, and with sincerity of heart, just as you would obey Christ. Obey them not only to win their favor when their eye is on you, but as slaves of Christ, doing the will of God from your heart. Serve wholeheartedly, as if you were serving the Lord, not people, because you know that the Lord will reward each one for whatever good they do, whether they are slave or free.**

Ephesians 6:5-8 NIV. Also, **1 Peter 2:18 NKJV** says: **Servants, be submissive to your masters with all fear, not only to the good and gentle, but also to the harsh**.

For the purpose of this book, I am going to endeavour not to use the word 'slaves' because I believe when you are a new creature, old things have passed away, you are no longer a slave, you are free through Christ. If Jesus took your curse and gave you freedom, why do you want to be carrying the curse you are delivered from? In this day and age, if you work for someone, you are entitled to get paid according to the agreement of your employment. I have seen many employees being treated as slaves in our time and it is called modern slavery. To work for many hours without a break or work for a full month and for the employer to delay the wages is slavery. To work for hours and not get paid or taken advantage of your flexibility and hard work is modern slavery. So, you are not a slave and should not expect to be treated as such. When conditions of employment change, do not be scared to ask why and seek advice on what to do. Do not suffer in silence. There are some things you tolerate because you are new in a job or you are trying to adjust to the new position but bullying, racism and abuse by your employer should not be tolerated as you are not helping the situation. We all have our part to play to bring justice into our workplace.

I work with people with learning difficulties and autism. I always make them understand that I am not a slave rather I am employed to support their basic needs. I believe if my clients understand the reason I am there it is easy for both of us to work together to achieve a positive result. I have worked with difficult clients whom the parent cannot even ask them to take their plate to the kitchen because they know that the reaction that will follow will not be pleasant. With these clients, I am not expecting a rapid change in their behaviour but a gradual and consistence approach when I explain properly that I am there to support will benefit them. My employer always commended the relationship I had with my client and my principle of 'I am not their slave but their support'. There is a difference, as I have seen other staff do a lot for their client and in the process they cripple the client. It is not helping but disabling them. In the 21st century; nannies, cleaners, carers, support workers are not slaves but professionals because their services are needed. A nanny and a doctor are both needed and they are employed by someone. For instance, the nanny can be employed by the doctor and the doctor can be employed by health services. However, there are some employers who still treat people as slaves. THIS IS IGNORANCE ON THEIR PART and they need to be educated. I have worked as a nanny and I must say I was treated extremely well by my employers. After paying my salary, my employer will go out of their way to show me how much they appreciated my service by buying me gifts/ vouchers, organised a pamper /spa day and hosted myself and my boys during festive periods. Slavery should not be tolerated and if you are being treated unfairly by your boss, talk to the Lord and get legal advice. Let the Holy Spirit give you wisdom on how to deal with the situation and let the Lord fight for you. Recently (2020), my employer refused to pay me for not working during the Covid19 pandemic due to my health condition. I left it in God's hand but unknown to me two ladies from head office made sure I got paid and my employer did pay me. To God be the glory. **Romans 12:17-19 NKJV says, "Repay no one evil for evil. Have regard for good things in the sight of all men. If it is possible, as much as depends on you, live peaceably with all men. Beloved, do not avenge yourselves, but rather give place to wrath; for it is written, "Vengeance is Mine, I will repay," says the Lord.** In some parts of the world, employees are still treated as slaves or trafficked as slaves. I pray the Lord will intervene on their behalf and avenge for them. The Lord knows that they are being mistreated and in due course He will come and rescue them. Weeping might be for a night but joy comes in the morning. Stay faithful and loyal to your employer but do not hesitate if you have to leave. **He said: "Listen, King Jehoshaphat and all who live in Judah and Jerusalem! This is what the Lord says to you: 'Do not be afraid or discouraged because of this vast army. For the battle is not yours, but God's (2 Chronicles 20:15).**

WHAT ARE MY RESPONSIBILITIES AS AN EMPLOYEE?

Obey your earthly masters with <u>respect</u> and <u>fear</u>, and with <u>sincerity of heart</u>, just as you would obey Christ. <u>Obey</u> them not only to win their favor when their eye is on you, but as slaves of Christ, doing the will of God from your heart. <u>Serve wholeheartedly</u>, as if you were serving the Lord, not people, because you know that the Lord will

reward each one for whatever good they do, whether they are slaves or free (Ephesians6:5-8).

OBEDIENCE: Obey your employer with respect, fear and sincerity of heart as you would obey Christ. When you start any job, you are given a job role, policies and guidelines of the work place. It is your responsibility as an employee to follow these. The consequences of not adhering to the company rules may lead to demotion, getting sacked, being fined, criminal record or a jail sentence if negligence is found. The perception of my company changed 2 years ago, when the holy spirit told me in one of my morning devotion that my complaining about what was wrong at my work place was not going to change unless I changed my thoughts. He told me I work for HIM not my employer. How? **"Then the righteous will answer Him, saying, 'Lord, when did we see You hungry and feed You, or thirsty and give You drink? When did we see You a stranger and take you in, or naked and clothe You? Or when did we see You sick, or in prison, and come to You?' And the King will answer and say to them, 'Assuredly, I say to You, in as much as you did it to one of the least of these My brethren, You did it to Me.' Matthew 25:37-40 NKJV.**You might be thinking but they are not Christians! It does not matter, the Lord put you in that place as an ambassador for Him. So therefore your conduct and character must honour and glorify Him. **Galatians6:10NKJV** tells us to do good to people especially when we have the opportunity to do so. Obey your employer not only to win their favour when their eyes are on you, but as doing the will of God from your heart." **"Bond servants, be obedient to**

those who are your masters according to the flesh, with fear and trembling, in sincerity of heart, as to Christ; not with eye service, as men-pleasers, but as bondservants of Christ, doing the will of God from the heart, with goodwill doing service, as to the Lord, and not to men, knowing that whatever good anyone does, he will receive the same from the Lord, whether he is a slave or free (Ephesians6:5-8NKJV). Most times, employees may not work directly with the owner of the business but work with those representing the owner i.e. Managers or senior management. Our duty as an ambassador for Christ is to obey them and do what is required for us as long as it is legal. If you do not agree with a task, bring it to your employer's attention and give a reason as to why you do not want to follow their requests. Years ago my manager asked me to take some clients to the park. Personally, I did not think the ratio of staff to client was right but also according to health and safety at work act, I did not think it is was safe and if anything happened while we were at the park, I would be liable. Discreetly, I went to the manager's office, stated my facts and told her that I will go to the park but if anything happened I would let the prosecutor know that I informed the manager of the dangers involved then I left her office. A few minutes later she came out and made alternative arrangements. Make complaints known to your employer without being aggressive or undermining employer's authority in public. Do it discreetly and in love as to the Lord. State the facts/ problem, suggest solutions and contribution /compromise you are willing to make and leave the rest to God to deal with.

RESPECT: I like the word **"RESPECT"** in **Ephesians 6**. Respect cannot be demanded, it needs to be earned. What do you say about your employer? Do you pray for your boss? What are your motives towards your employer? What is your contribution towards your company? Show respect not only to your employer alone but to everything that relates to your job/company. How do you treat the resources given to you? Integrity goes a long way. You cannot expect to be blessed if you turn up at work any time you like and leave before your contracted hours for no reason. You cannot be the only one with traffic and bus lateness excuses all the time. Stop making excuses and start making a difference. Above all, you claim to be a Christian or better still a pastor. How insulting is that in the face of Jehovah. Our Father was efficient, hardworking and on time. When He said let there be light, it appeared. He created heaven and earth in 6 days and rested on the 7th day. He did not leave what He was doing to take a break until it was finished and when it was completed, it was beautiful **(Genesis1)**. If you want your employer to respect you, turn up to work on time and leave work when you are supposed to. Do not dig a hole for yourself rather be wise to receive the honour and recognition for a good service. Haman thought he was being smart by advising the king the kind of honour to give the king's delight but it turned out that the person that was awarded the honour was the man Haman hated, a Jew and the man he had planned to hang him in the gallows but he ended in the gallows **(Esther5&6 KJV)**. Do not ignore your duty as an employee to mind anything that does not concern you or has any relevance to your job. Be a man of your word.

FEAR OF GOD: The fear of God is what makes us to serve wholeheartedly without pretence, deceit and hypocrisy. The Fear of God does not mean we are afraid of God, it means that we reverence who He is, honour Him and acknowledge Him in all our ways. The fear of God is what makes us to be sincere and come clean when we have done wrong. As believers, we need to be honest to confront and expose bad practice in the workplace. It might be a normal thing to lie but for believers we have a Father who sees in secret and will reward openly. These are common lies I have heard and seen in the workplace; a man had gone somewhere and did not turn up for his shift, when he finally turned up to work, he told an emotional lie that his mother (who had died over 20years ago) passed away. Another one was a pastor's wife who went to a church conference and told her employer she was not well. Do not be part of what is common to man but dishonour God. Reverence the Lord with all that you do.

Many years ago I had to choose between my two jobs due to health reasons. My friends were surprised that I chose the job that did not have many benefits and it was pay as you go. Deliberately I did not choose the other job for many reasons i.e. I wanted reduced hours to give my body time to heal, the sick pay would not help me thrive to recover because every time I was not well I stayed home but when I didn't work, I knew there will be no pay so I pulled myself together and went to work and God gave me favour with my employer and colleagues. Daniel purposed in his heart that he will not defile himself by eating and drinking from the king delicacies and the Lord granted him favour with the official in charge of the young men **(Daniel1:8-9).** When you honour God with what you have God will bless you, you might be thinking; but why is that relevant to you choosing the job? My body is the temple of God and what I do with it matters to Him. **Do you not know that your bodies are temples of the Holy Spirit, who is in you, whom you have received from God? You are not your own; you were bought at a price. Therefore honor God with your bodies (1Corinthians6:19-20).**The Holy Spirit is ever so present and will help us to reject bad habit in the workplace if we are willing to change and do things in God's way.

SINCERITY OF HEART: Sincerity means you do things without pretence, deceit and hypocrisy. Our world today is full of this these three. The fact that you have thousands of followers on social media does not mean all of them like you. People do things for selfish reasons these days and unfortunately the workplace is not exempted from this kind of behaviour and practices. As believers, we should not be conformed to the things of this world but be transformed by the renewing of our mind, being able to test and approve God's good and perfect will **(Romans 12:2).** Have a sincerity of heart when you are not being watched. Be faithful when your employer is not present. Remember that the Lord is watching you even though your employer might not. I WOULD RATHER FEAR THE ONE WHO SEES IN THE SECRET THAN THE ONE WHO SEES IN THE OPEN. Sometimes when am doing something at work and the Holy Spirit says; if your employer is here now, will you do that? Straightaway, I stop whatever it is I was doing, ask the

Lord to forgive me and refuse to do it again. I am still a work in progress and I know sometimes I forget and old habits start coming back but once the Holy Spirit convicts me, I know it is time to change. Our Father never gives up on us no matter how many times we fail. He judges the heart and once our heart is clean as **Psalms51:10-12** declares, then we are in the right standing with God. The bible tells us that while we were yet a sinner Christ died for us **(Romans5:8),** all we need to do is to make sure that His death is not in vain. The employer might not see but the Lord sees and the one who sees in secret will reward me openly.

When I babysit for friends, even though they are my boss, when they are not around, the kids become my boss, I treat them as if their parents are in front of me. Sometimes, when the kids and I have a misunderstanding, I text the parent to explain what happened, where I was wrong and where I had to apologise to the child even before they got home. When we start treating our bosses right, even those who treat us with disrespect, the Lord will fight for us. **"Who then is the faithful and wise servant, whom the master has put in charge of the servants in his household to give them their food at the proper time? It will be good for that servant whose master finds him doing so when he returns. Truly I tell you, he will put him in charge of all his possessions (Matthew 24:45-47).**

SERVE WHOLEHEARTEDLY: Serve wholeheartedly, as if you were serving the Lord, not people, because you know that the Lord will reward each one for whatever good they do,

whether they are slave or free (Ephesians6:7-8).Serve your employer with everything you have. Serve as if it is your business. Serve God not man. Serve like your life depends on it. Serve as you would serve your pastor. Your responsibility as an employee is not separated from your responsibility as a child of God. Jesus told a story about a man who went on a journey but before he went he gave his servants bags of gold. To one he gave 5bags, 2bags to another and 1bag to another, each according to their abilities. When the master came back from his trip he was surprised to find out that 2 servants had doubled the value of what they were given: **"His master replied, 'Well done, good and faithful servant! You have been faithful with a few things; I will put you in charge of many things. Come and share your master's happiness!' (Matthew 25:21).** What do you think the master said to the servant he gave one bag of gold and he hid it in the ground instead of investing it? **"His master replied, 'You wicked, lazy servant! So you knew that I harvest where I have not sown and gather where I have not scattered seed? Well then, you should have put my money on deposit with the bankers, so that when I returned I would have received it back with interest. 'So take the bag of gold from him and give it to the one who has ten bags. For whoever has will be given more, and they will have an abundance. Whoever does not have, even what they have will be taken from them. And throw that worthless servant outside, into the darkness, where there will be weeping and gnashing of teeth.' (Matthew25:26-30).**Why did the servant hid the money of his master? He was afraid that what he knew about his master might come to pass. His fear brought his downfall **(Matthew25:24-25)**. What do you know about your workplace? What are you afraid of about your job? What have you heard or been told about your company?

Be faithful at all times because you do not know when the reward will come. Do not just turn up to work for the sake of the money but turn up with an aim to make your colleagues, clients, manager, supervisors happy. Do not just work but be productive. Do to others what you will want others to do for you. Your work environment might still be the same when you choose to be different but believe you are serving the Lord. Decide to make a different approach today and quit grumbling and complaining about things you cannot control. Be positive even when you cannot see the road at the end of the tunnel. I learnt from a pastor years ago that the best thing you can do for a leader is to be positive and a problem solver rather than create it. Make huge problems become smaller. Be a solution not a problem. I must confess that there was a time in my life when my emotions were controlled by my feelings. Moaning and complaining at work used to be my thing especially if things did not seem right. Let's just say my confrontation skills were zero but I had to learn how to express myself in a calm and loving way for my employer to understand. My actions were based on what I was dealing with myself i.e. low self-esteem, pride, arrogance, jealous, envy, un-forgiveness and the feeling of not being appreciated. Through some training at work, I had to learn how to be assertive and say no without feeling guilty.

Years ago in my previous job, I decided to change my communication skills and stop complaining/gossip to my colleagues about my boss. If I had any issues relating to work, I would go to my boss privately and express my view about the matter. Most of the time it is a misunderstanding. The scripture says, a calm spirit turns away wrath (**Proverb15:1**). I must admit the changes were difficult at the beginning as it was the norm among staff to blame the manager for everything but as I continued to praise my boss, acknowledge what she did and prayed for her, my boss's attitude changed towards me. When I was leaving the job, she commented on the things I had suggested while working for her and said that she would start to put them into practice. Years have gone by and she is still asking my friend if I want to come back to work for her. Recently, I went to their Christmas party and I was welcomed by those who knew me and those who had heard about me. To God be the glory.

Do not repay evil with evil or insult with insult. On the contrary, repay evil with blessing, because to this you were called so that you may inherit a blessing. For, "Whoever would love life and see good days must keep their tongue from evil and their lips from deceitful speech. They must turn from evil and do good; they must seek peace and pursue it (1 Peter 3:9-11).

If you are an employee today that is not all you can be. You should have the mind set to become an employer or do your own thing one day. I work for an employer but I have other things that I do that satisfy me. Even though I am doing my own thing by the side, I am loyal, faithful and steadfast to my employer. I have a principle; whatever I do when I have nothing is the same thing I will do on my way to where I am going. For example, the way I treated the one room is the same way I treated two rooms when I got them.

The way I treated the two rooms is the same way I am treating my two bedroom flat until I move into my own house. One thing a lot of people do not realise is that when I moved into our one room, the land lady did not agree with the agent, (I think she did not want someone with children) and she made it known by her actions but we ended up staying at the property until she wanted to sell. Even when she found a buyer she delayed it until we found a place to rent. When you obey, respect, reverence God and serve wholeheartedly with a sincere heart there is reward for your service. Be a good employee.

PRAYER/CONFESSION

Lord, I am grateful for the opportunity to offer my service to others. I do realise that many do not have work at the moment. So, I am thankful for Your provision

I ask for God's forgiveness for every time I have complained about my job or employer. May I always praise and appreciate my employer for what they do. I choose to pray for them rather than complain about them.

I will persevere to be the employee that God wants me to be and give my best even if I am not recognised for it.

Holy Spirit help me to be prudent at all times and let my service be pleasing to God. May I paint pictures of success not defeat. May I pleasure in doing what is right. I am grateful that I get paid for what I do.

I invite patience into my work etiquette and I refuse unnecessary pressure that causes distractions and failure.

I partner with love not hate and I choose peace over pain. I choose plain and simple over plain and foolishness and store plenty not waste. I refuse to pick on every fault but pick on every achievement. I will not be a partaker of evil but a partaker of good. I will be positive rather than be pessimistic. I will be passionate with the tasks given to me rather than being passive. I will protect my employer and workplace and not destroy them. I will be persistent not pathetic. My protection over clients will not turn to being possessive over them. I will be polite to colleagues not pompous.

I loose myself from every situation that has kept me bound for years. I remove heavy burdens that I have carried from centuries or my fore fathers, pain passed from generation to generation. Every yoke in my destiny is destroyed in Jesus's name. Everything that has consumed me or eaten up my harvest will be removed. The Lord will restore to me the years that the locust, cankerworm, caterpillar, palmerworm has eaten **(Joel2:25).** I completely destroy anything that represent the Hittites, Amorites, Canaanites, Perizzites, Hivites and Jebusites in my life **(Deuteronomy20:17)**

I will not only consume but I will produce wealth to nations. I will not be a victim but a victor. I will not just be a receiver but I will give and lend to many nations. I will not settle for handouts or pass on but stand tall on my feet with my head lifted high.

Abimelech came to Isaac because he was afraid of him and did not want Isaac to harm him **(Genesis 26:28-29).** When God elevates me, my enemy will come to make peace with me. Those who have cursed me will come and rejoice at my promotion. Those who have cursed my God because of my situation will salute my God when my breakthrough comes, they will say plainly the Lord is with me.

EMPLOYER

In this chapter, I want to draw our attention to how the Lord wants us to treat the people He puts under us to manage in order for them to reach their maximum potential. The way you treat people God has placed under you matters to Him, He created them all even the odd ones who decide to be difficult and ungrateful. He will reward them for their deeds accordingly. Cain brought his offering and so did Abel but God favoured Abel's offering and did not look at Cain's offering with favour **(Genesis 4:3-5).** God searches all hearts and he rewards those who are faithful and diligent to Him. It is important to treat your employee in the same way you want your employer to treat you. **And masters, treat your slaves in the same way. Do not threaten them, since you know that he who is both their master and yours is in heaven, and there is no favouritism with him (Ephesians 6:9**). In this verse, Paul helped us to see what the Lord required of employers as they serve their employees. He said to treat them the same way that they expect the employee to treat them in obedience, respect, with a sincere heart, the fear God and serve wholeheartedly as Christ did when he was on earth.

As followers of Christ created in the image of God, our characters or attitude towards others must portray the one who made us in his image. Right! I know it is not easy to lead /manage things not to mention to manage people, the Lord knows it too. Remember He called the children of Israel stiff-necked people **(Exodus32:9). There is a reason why Solomon asked God to give him wisdom to govern his**

people Israel (1King3:5-9). To be a leader or employer that God wants you to be, you are going to need God's wisdom. Congratulations to every employer/leader reading this book. I want to thank you for the work you do and I pray that God will bless you abundantly. In my life, I learnt most of my leadership skills through looking after my kids and it is not easy. I have to rely on the Holy Spirit to help me. When the Lord started putting people in my path to mentor/lead, I struggled as I find it difficult to relate with adults as they are set in their ways. With children, they are still learning and growing and you can still teach them one or two things and they will listen. As an adult, I am set in my ways but everyday I learn to accommodate other people in order to live in this world. No matter what you do, there will be some people you cannot help, just do your part to honour God and leave the rest for Him. In the Garden of Eden there was the tree of life and the tree of the knowledge of good and evil. Just like in the garden, in the workplace or among the people you lead, there are bound to be those who will not follow orders or respect what you are thriving to achieve and this is what Proverbs says about those people.

Like snow in summer or rain in harvest, honor is not fitting for a fool. Like a fluttering sparrow or a darting swallow, an undeserved curse does not come to rest. A whip for the horse, a bridle for the donkey, and a rod for the backs of fools! Do not answer a fool according to his folly, or you yourself will be just like him. Answer a fool according to his folly, or he will be wise in his own eyes. Sending a message by the hands of a fool is

like cutting off one's feet or drinking poison. Like the useless legs of one who is lame is a proverb in the mouth of a fool. Like tying a stone in a sling is the giving of honor to a fool. Like a thornbush in a drunkard's hand is a proverb in the mouth of a fool. Like an archer who wounds at random is one who hires a fool or any passer-by. As a dog returns to its vomit, so fools repeat their folly. Do you see a person wise in their own eyes? There is more hope for a fool than for them (Proverbs26:1-12). Stubborn people who repeatedly refuse to accept correction will suddenly be broken and never recover (Proverbs29:1TPT). You Can't Argue with a Fool. Arrogant cynics love to pick fights, but the humble and wise love to pursue peace. There's no use arguing with a fool, for his ranting and raving prevent you from making a case and settling the argument in a calm way. Violent men hate those with integrity, but the lovers of God esteem those who are holy. You can recognize fools by the way they give full vent to their rage and let their words fly! But the wise bite their tongue and hold back all they could say (Proverbs29:8-11 TPT). A rebellious fool will despise your wise advice, so don't even waste your time—save your breath! (Proverbs23:9TPT)

Let us look at Moses's story as a leader. He delivered the Israelites from slavery and their captor. One time out of many times the people were thirsty for water and they grumbled against Moses. "Why did you bring us up out of Egypt to make us, our children and livestock die of thirst?" They asked, **(Exodus 17:3)**. After being delivered from poverty and slavery, this was their response every time they faced obstacles. It got so bad at one time that God had to interrupt their conversation on Mount Sinai. Moses had gone for forty days and forty nights to be in the presence of God to receive instruction on how to live in the land that God promised them and the people thought Moses was long gone, they gathered around Aaron and said, **"Come, make us gods who will go before us. As for this fellow Moses who brought us up out of Egypt, we don't know what has happened to him." Then the Lord said to Moses, "Go down, because your people, whom you brought up out of Egypt, have become corrupt. (Exodus 32:1, 7)."** Being an employer means you own the business or you are managing it for someone else or acting on behalf of someone. While managing comes natural with some people, some have to learn to fit in the position. Employers are either good or bad based on their leadership, communication and relational skills. That is why the majority of employers attend various training courses to help them in their position because nothing prepares you for the challenges you face when you actually step into that position.

Whether you are a leader or employer, it is important to treat those under you in the right way because you WILL answer to God. Do not settle issues between your employees based on hearsay or listen only to one side of the story. Let your judgement be fair. Do not create enmity between those you lead. You can prefer one person from another but don't treat two employees differently it only causes envy and jealousy **(James2).** We have seen different stories in the bible where one person is favoured more than the other i.e.

Jacob and Esau **(Genesis 25:27-28)**; Ismael and Isaac **(Genesis16)**; Hannah and Peninnah **(1Samuel1)**; Lea and Rachel **(Genesis 30)**. Favouritism only causes frictions, hatred, bitterness and resentment. Be a peacemaker among those God has put under you. My present manager is just a God sent for so many reasons. She is not a Christian but she listens to her staff and makes sure she looks after the welfare of her staff and clients. There is nothing you need that she will not provide. Her kindness creates peace in the home and a good working environment. She is not one sided in handling situations between staff, she listens and tries as much as possible in her power to make her staff and clients happy. In return staff turn up for work on time. When she was sick, staff rallied round her, ran the home well that she didn't have to worry about what was happening in the home in her absence, which helped her speedy recovery. **When leaders listen to false accusations, their associates become scoundrels. Poor people and their oppressors have only one thing in common—God made them both. The best insurance for a leader's longevity is to demonstrate justice for the poor. Experiencing many corrections and rebukes will make you wise (Proverbs29:12-15TPT).**

I have witnessed leaders/managers ignore behaviour that was affecting everyone in the workplace simply because of their own motives i.e. they liked the person who was causing problems and wanted a relationship with them, or they come from the same country or they are family members/friends or to despise someone who didn't positively respond to them when they declared their feelings towards the person. Do not be a bully or misuse your authority. God will not be pleased with you and the cry of an innocent person who suffers the consequences of your actions rises to heaven and in due time you will get the judgement you deserve. The bible says; p**ay close attention to the teaching that corrects you, and open your heart to every word of instruction. Don't withhold appropriate discipline from your child. Go ahead and punish him when he needs it. Don't worry—it won't kill him! A good spanking could be the very thing that teaches him a lifelong lesson! My beloved child, when your heart is full of wisdom, my heart is full of gladness. And when you speak anointed words, we are speaking mouth to mouth! Don't allow the actions of evil men to cause you to burn with anger. Instead, burn with unrelenting passion as you worship God in holy awe (Proverbs23:12-17TPT).**Do not take advantage of those who work for you. Pay them the right wage on time. They have worked and they expect to be paid as they have to pay their bills. I have worked for an employer who would go on holiday without paying staff or would just not pay on the day he was meant to or he would pay two days late with no concrete explanation as to why he delayed the payment. The bible says; **never move a long-standing boundary line or attempt to take land that belongs to the fatherless. For they have a mighty protector, a loving redeemer, who watches over them, and he will stand up for their cause (Proverbs23:10-11TPT).**

There are a few things that I want to draw to your attention to as we look at employers/leaders. These are leadership skills, communication skills, partnership, training and the fear of God

LEADERSHIP SKILLS: A leader is someone who influences or motivates a group of people to achieve a goal. This can only be achieved if he or she knows what she/he is doing. What is your style of leadership? Is it dictatorship, friendly, bossy, flexible? Do you retain or force your employees to leave? Do you have principles? What is your objective? What gets you out of bed in the morning? What are you looking for? What gets your attention? What ticks your box? What arouses your desire? What pushes your buttons? What triggers your excitement? What makes you who you are? I am not an expert on the subject, but I am trying to make you think about who you are and should be. There are books and training courses on the subject that will help you to become a better employer. As an employer, you need to choose the right style of leading and manage your employees with RESPECT. **"Tell Aaron and his sons to treat with respect the sacred offerings the Israelites consecrate to me, so they will not profane my holy name. I am the Lord (Leviticus 22:2).** The people working for you or working under you are sacred to the Lord, treat them right. They have sacrificed their time and are expected to receive a reward.

COMMUNICATION SKILLS: HOW DO YOU COMMUNICATE WITH YOUR EMPLOYEE? What comes to your mind when you are talking to your employee? Potential, progress, promotion, failure, success, problems, slaves, animals, liability? Do you listen to your employee or you just dish out tasks? If you do not love yourself you cannot love other people. What you have is what you can give others. Love cannot give birth to hate.

The wise store up knowledge, but the mouth of a fool invites ruin (Proverbs 10:14).

Be wise in the way you act toward outsiders; make the most of every opportunity. Let your conversation be always full of grace, seasoned with salt, so that you may know how to answer everyone (Colossians 4:5-6 NIV)

PARTNERSHIP: Work together with your employees. You need them as much as they need you. When building a house you need every expertise to work on the architectural plan. Your cleaner is as important as the manager. Get your employees involved in your business, encourage them to have an input and use their gift and talent productively. Recognise and acknowledge workers who are diligent, hardworking, honest, loyal and flexible. Do not look down or ignore someone because they are not educated or intelligent as you. The bible says one will chase a thousand and two will put ten thousand to flight **(Deuteronomy32:30 KJV).** Do not underestimate the contribution of the least important. If you don't appreciate and recognize your employee's contribution you will lose them and it will affect your turnover. Treat others how you like to be treated. At the end of the day, when you sleep at night, be happy that you have done your best for your employees. You cannot please everyone but you can please the majority. Listen, learn from your employees and create an atmosphere for criticism and feedback. That is the way to grow your business. **For he who does wrong will be punished for his wrongdoing, and [with God] there is no partiality [no special treatment based on a person's position in life].Colossians 3:25 AMP**

TRAINING: Train and learn more to be a better employer. Challenge yourself. Be creative. You don't know everything. I have worked for a manager who kept my job for 6 month when I was recovering from an illness even though I was only a bank staff. So, what you do does not go unnoticed. I have also worked for a manager who did not care about me and treated me as if I didn't matter. **The fear of the Lord is the beginning of knowledge, but fools despise wisdom and instruction. (Proverbs 1:7).**

Then you will understand the fear of the Lord and find the knowledge of God. For the Lord gives wisdom; from his mouth come knowledge and understanding. He holds success in store for the upright, he is a shield to those whose walk is blameless, for he guards the course of the just and protects the way of his faithful ones (Proverbs 2:5-8).

Let the people who work for you or work under you know your vision and plan for the business so that they can know how to run with it. The Lord told Habakkuk to **"Write the vision. And engrave it plainly on [clay] tablets. So that the one who reads it will run (Habakkuk2:2AMP).** The reason why policies and procedures are in the workplace is for the staff to follow them. Let your employees know what you stand for. If you are hardworking, your employees will follow suit. Integrity, flexibility, loyalty and prudence rubs off from the top. Let your employer see Jesus in you and through you. I cherish my landlord and his family so much because of the way he treats me and my children. Anytime we call upon him for repairs he gets on it straight away. Sometimes I do not want to bother him unless it is necessary. He is truly a child of God compared to where I have come from. The previous land lady was a Christian too but we were walking on eggshells especially when she was around. She did not appreciate the effort we put into obeying the rules, cleaning and keeping the house tidy. All she did was complain and never gave me back my deposit for the house when we moved OUT. It is important to let people know that there are consequences when they step out of line and break the rules. Always make sure you follow through with what you have planned. There is a story in Matthew 18 about a master who forgave his servant and wrote off the debt he had but when the same servant came across his fellow servant who only owed him few hundreds he did not do the same for him. He threw him in the prison and when his master heard of it this is what he said:

"Then the master called the servant in. 'You wicked servant,' he said, 'I cancelled all that debt of yours because you begged me to. Shouldn't you have had mercy on your fellow servant just as I had on you? 'In anger his master handed him over to the jailers to be tortured, until he should

pay back all he owed."This is how my heavenly Father will treat each of you unless you forgive your brother or sister from your heart."(Matthew18:32-35)

There are six things the Lord hates, seven that are detestable to him: haughty eyes, a lying tongue, hands that shed innocent blood, a heart that devises wicked schemes, feet that are quick to rush into evil, a false witness who pours out lies and a person who stirs up conflict in the community(Proverbs 6:16-19)

If you spend millions on training and you don't provide the right environment for that training to be utilized, the money is wasted. If you do not invest in your employees, your business will struggle.

FEAR OF GOD

Serve your employees with the fear of God. Know that you are being watched. They are not a commodity. **Masters, [on your part] deal with your slaves justly and fairly, knowing that you also have a master in heaven. Be persistent and devoted to prayer, being alert and focused in your prayer life with an attitude of thanksgiving (Colossians 4:1-2 AMP).** There are consequences for not treating your employees in the right way. Whatever you sow, you will harvest. If you treat your employees well, things will go well with you. During the Covid19 pandemic, some managers praised their employees for going beyond their duty of care by turning up to work knowing that they might go home with the virus which was a sacrifice and a risk to their family. Some went knowing there was no protective clothing.

I heard about employees who did not expect to get paid for the extra hours they worked. Some even volunteered their time, knowing fully well that their employers could not even afford to pay them. The response from workers was phenomenal simply because the employer has been good to them.

PRAYER AND CONFESSION

I am grateful and thankful for counting me worthy to serve those You have put under me to manage and lead.

The bible says, if anyone lacks wisdom they should ask **(James1:5).** I ask for wisdom, knowledge, understanding, discretion and discernment to lead in the way that is right before God.

Father, I ask for forgiveness in any way that I have treated my employee unfairly and unjustly. Show me and teach me Your ways and give me the strength to follow Your instructions. Give me courage and boldness to stand for what is right. Let me be a good role model for others to follow. Bring my way employees that have good intentions for my business. Employees that will ruin and destroy my business will not come to me. Expose any hidden agenda that will cause harm to me, my business or the people that work for me. I receive employees that are faithful, loyal, hardworking, flexible, intelligent, understanding, creative, willing to learn, change and accept correction.

When I am looking for someone to work for me or partner with me, Lord give me insight, may I not just look at the outward appearance alone but be discerning to know who is best suitable for my business.

Give me wisdom to motivate talents and gifts. Let me appreciate and give recognition to those that work for me. I will not work hard to build my business for someone else to reap the reward. I release over my business the spirit of love, joy peace, tolerance, endurance, faith, meekness, kindness, patience and generosity. Always show me the best way to lead, communicate and relate to those under me. May I not undermine the effort from each member of my staff. You are Lord of all and You see all things, reveal to me any areas that need change and improvement. I place my business into Your hands, it is Yours Lord, I am just hands and feet that carry out Your assignment on earth. Let the image of my business portray who you are. Let this business open doors for miracles, signs and wonders, salvation, opportunities and success. Let it attract great influences. You are the one who creates wealth and add no sorrow to it. Let this business create wealth that will support the gospel of Your son Jesus Christ.

The Israelites did not come out of Egypt empty handed, my business will not come out empty handed will come out with blessings, favour, opportunities, prosperity and promotion. It will flourish

Many people followed the Israelites when they were coming out of Egypt because the people feared their God. I ask that my day of victory will attract many to the God that I serve. What I have acquired in the days of weeping will be enough to feed me and my family. I will not be a follower of someone's dreams. I will not run someone's race but I will run my race from the start to the finish. I will not stop or collapse in the middle of my race. I will not carry the burdens that were meant for my enemies. I will not be a borrower but a lender. I will be fruitful and increase greatly wherever I go.

During the famine in Egypt, every land was sold apart from the one that belonged to the Priest **(Genesis47:22).** My blessings will not be taken from me because of arrogance and pride. My position will not be taken from me because of ignorance. Great opportunities will not be taken from me because of foolishness. My investment will yield a harvest.

Goshen was a foreign land for the Israelites but they acquired property. I will acquire great wealth and riches in a foreign land.

Every curses known and unknown have been removed from my life. I have freedom and victory; so therefore, I receive the dew of heaven. I receive the fatness of the earth. I receive plenty of grain. I receive new wine. I receive a new beginning. Old things have passed away and I receive the new things You are doing in my life. I refuse old information that is not working for me and receive new career/ business/ projects opportunities, promotion, joy and peace. Oh

Lord, Bless the work of my hands. Send destiny helpers and miracle workers to me. **(Genesis27:28)**

I will not want for the Lord is my Shepherd. He will supply all my needs and protect everything that concerns me. As Isaac planted seeds in famine and reaped same year hundred times, I will reap plenty and hundred times in the land. I will become great and gain more and more until I become very wealthy and extremely distinguished **(Gen26:12-14)**

I will be blessed and highly favoured in the season of draught. As Isaac dug a well until the philistines could not contend with him no more and called it Rehoboth **(Gen26:15-22),** I will persevere, be resilient and not give up on the way of fulfilling my dreams. The Lord will make room for me and I will be fruitful in the land. When my enemy throws dirt into my work and laugh at me, I will be patient and allow the Lord to fight my battle, for I know I have overcome by the blood of the lamb and by the word of my testimony **(Rev12:11).** When people forget what I have done for them in the past, become hostile to me and forget to keep their promise, help me to be at peace and know that God will be with me and make a way for me.

RECOMMENDATIONS

This includes some songs, movies, talk shows, books and messages that help me on my journey of faith

SONGS

Dunsin Oyekan- Breathe

Nataliel Bassey- Onise Iyanu(awesome wonder)

Tabernacle choir- Psalm 23

Hillsong United- As You find me. Starts and Ends

William McDowell - Withholding nothing. Don't mind waiting

William Mcdowell, Travis Greene& Nataniel Bassey-Nothing like your presence

Cory Asbury- Reckless love

House of Heroes worship- Come Holy Spirit

Integrity music worship- Pure Heart; Almighty; I will rejoice;

Ron Kenoly- Lift Him Up

Don Moen- Give Thanks

Benjamin Dube- Bow down and worship Him

Hosanna scripture memory songs: God's love, I will praise you, Provision, Forgiveness, Overcoming fear, Overcoming stress, God's promises, Renewing your mind

Michael W Smith- Heart of God

Donnie Mcclurkin- Holy; Stand; Praise, Hymns & Spiritual

Maverick City- Jireh, Promises, Refiner

MESSAGES

Owen McManus- 21/01/20 Hillsong London podcast

Ray Bevan – 12/01/20 Hillsong UK podcast

Dr Robi - Dads and Lads

Gary Clarke- When the son comes home 13/09/2015 father's day message 21/6/2020 (you tube)

Robbie Lewis Hillsong- shame13/4/19, Hillsong London podcast

Ben bluebell Hillsong - One day at a time, 02/08/2020 Hillsong London podcast

SY Roger- Areal life experience, Sexual brokenness

Jackie Hill Perry- Gay Girl, Good God; Discovering the truth about identity; Sexuality and identity; My story and How God Saved Me

Mental Wealth- Ana Loback & Gary Clarke (you tube)

Td jakes-Stay on track 2015 (you tube)

Myles Munroe - Relationships

Matthew Ashimolowo - morning glow, life class, Wednesday bible study 2020 (check you tube)

Nomthi Odukoya- 2021 mother's day conversation with Pastor Nomthi – single, married, waiting and adoption

Taiwo odukoya – Messages 2020/21

Tolu Ella dara - True talk 2019-2020 (check you tube)

Gloria & Kenneth Copeland 2001 to 2020 messages (check you tube)

Bimbo Odukoya- Marriages & Single & Relationships

Books

Brian Houston – Live, Love, Lead

Dr Gary Smalley/ Ted Cunningham- from Anger to intimacy

Matthew Ashimolowo - War against poverty, The Power of positive confession volume 2, The Power of positive prayer bible

Gloria and Kenneth Copeland - Faith that moves mountain

T. D. Jakes- Identity, So you call yourself a man, **Judah Smith –** Love like Jesus

Ray Bevan- Grace shout louder. The Shack- WM. Paul Young

John C. Maxwell - The 5 Level of leadership

Jeremy Courtney- Pre-emptive Love

Myles Munroe – Men, Marriage, Fatherhood, Kingdom Parenting, Waiting & Dating, Understand the process of fasting, Prayer & Fasting consecration

Denzel Eboji - My journey from the speech therapist to the west end

MOVIES/ TV SHOWS:

War room

Overcomer

I can only imagine

Kingdom men rising

The shack, Left behind

Shield, Battleship

The Avengers

Iron lady

Man of steel

The last ship

Lost

Designated survivors

The 100

Air force one

Chosen.

Printed in Great Britain
by Amazon